"Most conversations, let alone ones about God, are either dull, single-sided or competing monologues full of smoke. It simply shouldn't be. Carrying on a vital, passionate, engaging conversation with another human being is an art that has been sufficiently lost that we need wisdom and perspective on how to engage well. *The God Conversation* is a gift to the church to invigorate our conversations with believers, seekers and unbelievers. J. P. and Tim walk with us through the use of story and authenticity with such masterful delight that one ends by sensing the authors have given us the very gift we are to give to others."

DAN B. ALLENDER, PRESIDENT AND PROFESSOR OF COUNSELING, MARS HILL GRADUATE SCHOOL; AUTHOR OF *THE WOUNDED HEART* AND *TO BE TOLD*

"Today's culture is increasingly a story-based culture. As Tim and J. P. help to show, a story-based culture does not have to be a culture without truth. This book is an excellent tool to learn how to better communicate the great truths about God, the world, our faith and human nature through stories, modern-day parables, and by listening and teaching like Jesus. It is a must-read for all who want to help others find faith in Jesus Christ."

ALAN ANDREWS, U.S. PRESIDENT, THE NAVIGATORS

"I love stories and illustrations because of the impact they have had on me. If they have had a similar effect on you, this book is for you. It will reinforce your faith, hone your ability to share your relationship to Jesus Christ and delight your imagination. I cannot give it a higher recommendation."

CLYDE COOK, FORMER PRESIDENT, BIOLA U

D0354742

"If you are a headhunting evangelist or an intellectual who must have the last word, put this book down and go home. If you love your pre-Christian friends and want stimulating resources to engage them in meaningful spiritual dialogue on hard questions, J. P. and Tim are the mentors you seek."

FRED H. WEVODAU, DIRECTOR, U.S. METRO MISSION, THE NAVIGATORS

"Moreland and Muehlhoff have written a unique and engaging book. The style is casual, yet the topics are treated with sufficient detail and nuance to be helpful. I commend *The God Conversation* to anyone seeking to discuss these matters in meaningful ways with family, friends and colleagues."

STAN W. WALLACE, NATIONAL DIRECTOR, FACULTY MINISTRY & EMERGING SCHOLARS NETWORK, INTERVARSITY CHRISTIAN FELLOWSHIP

The God Conversation

USING STORIES AND ILLUSTRATIONS TO EXPLAIN YOUR FAITH

J. P. Moreland & Tim Muehlhoff

Foreword by Lee Strobel

IVP Books

An imprint of InterVarsity Press
Downers Grove, Illinois

InterVarsity Press
P.O. Box 1400, Downers Grove, IL 60515-1426
World Wide Web: www.ivpress.com
E-mail: email@ivpress.com

InterVarsity Press® is the book-publishing division of InterVarsity Christian Fellowship/USA®, a student movement active on campus at hundreds of universities, colleges and schools of nursing in the United States of America, and a member movement of the International Fellowship of Evangelical Students. For information about local and regional activities, write Public Relations Dept., InterVarsity Christian Fellowship/USA, 6400 Schroeder Rd., P.O. Box 7895, Madison, WI 53707-7895, or visit the IVCF website at <www.intervarsity.org>.

All Scripture quotations, unless otherwise indicated, are taken from the Holy Bible, New International Version®. NIV®. Copyright ©1973, 1978, 1984 by International Bible Society. Used by permission of Zondervan Publishing House. All rights reserved.

Design: Cindy Kiple
Images: Mel Curtis/ Getty Images
Photodisc/ Getty Images
ISBN 978-0-8308-3489-1

Printed in the United States of America ∞

 InterVarsity Press is committed to protecting the environment and to the responsible use of natural resources. As a member of the Green Press Initiative we use recycled paper whenever possible. To learn more about the Green Press Initiative, visit <www.greenpressinitiative.org>.

Library of Congress Cataloging-in-Publication Data

Moreland, James Porter, 1948-
The God conversation: using stories and illustrations to explain
your faith / J. P. Moreland, Tim Muehlhoff.
    p. cm.
Includes bibliographical references and index.
ISBN-13: 978-0-8308-3489-1 (pbk.: alk. paper)
1. Apologetics—Methodology. 2. Storytelling—Religious
aspects—Christianity. I. Muehlhoff, Tim 1961- II. Title.
BT1103.M66 2007
239—dc22

                                                                                    2007026754

P   21   20   19   18   17   16   15   14   13   12   11   10

Y   24   23   22   21   20   19   18   17   16   15   14

Contents

Acknowledgments

We would like to thank all of our colleagues and friends at Biola University who read our manuscript as it progressed and offered invaluable insight and encouragement: Jon Lunde, Matt Williams, Erik Thoennes, Dave Horner, Mike Longinow, V. J. Vonk and Stacy Mushakian. We appreciate you!

I (Tim Muehlhoff) would like to especially thank the students of my Social Forms class (Spring 2006) who gladly served as a captive audience of early drafts of this material and offered honest insight, support and prayer for this project. Special shout out to Matt Scolinos for refining the title. Thanks to Todd Lewis for being eager about this project start to finish and helping me research and craft illustrations. Your door was always open! *As always,* I am grateful for a wife who listened to a thousand illustrations that didn't work, yet always believed in my skills and vision. Noreen, you are an illustration of love, support and partnership.

I (J. P. Moreland) would like to thank the Eidos Christian Center for help in providing me the time to work on this manuscript. Thanks also to my brothers and sisters at Anaheim Vineyard Church for being the sort of fellowship in which I experience the love of Jesus and the power of his kingdom. I am also grateful to those in ACSI for giving me a venue in which to try out some of the ideas in this manuscript. Finally, thanks to my friends in the Evangelical Philosophical Society for being examples of faithful, intelligent disciples of the Lord Jesus who earnestly try to help people understand why Jesus is, indeed, the Way, the Truth and the Life. I am especially grateful to Craig Hazen for the depth of his thought, the quality of his life and the passion he constantly exhibits for the Great Commission.

Foreword

More than a decade ago, I invited one of the authors of this book, J. P. Moreland, to Willow Creek Community Church to give a talk on science and faith. At the end of his presentation, a spiritual skeptic challenged him by saying that miracles overturn the laws of nature and therefore are impossible.

"Actually," said Moreland, "the laws of nature are the way we describe how the world usually works. If someone drops an apple, it falls to the floor. That's gravity. However, if someone were to drop an apple and I were to reach over and grab it before it hit the ground, I wouldn't be overturning the law of gravity. I would simply be intervening. In a similar way, God is able to reach into the world that he created by performing a miracle. He isn't contravening or overturning the laws of nature; he's simply intervening."

Moreland said a lot of brilliant things that evening. I recall being impressed with his entire presentation. But all these years later, his simple illustration of the falling apple is what I remember most clearly. That's what good illustrations do: they bring abstract concepts to life, heighten our interest and stick in our minds for long periods of time.

When I became a teaching pastor at Willow Creek, the power of good illustrations quickly became evident to me. As I would recite dry data in my sermons, people would sit back in their seats. When I would launch into an extended explanation of an issue, they seemed to relax. But when I would use a colorful example, a compelling story or an illuminating anecdote, they would sit up, move to the edge of their seats and lean forward. Their body language said it all: illustrations captivate people. No wonder Jesus told so many parables!

Moreland and his coauthor Tim Muehlhoff have done us a tremendous service by compiling this fascinating and practical volume. They've drawn upon a lifetime of experience to offer illustrations on a wide range of topics, from the problem of evil to world religions to the resurrection to ethics to the existence of God.

The God Conversation brims with creative material for your spiritual discussions with friends, neighbors, colleagues and family members. You'll find it to be an invaluable resource as you effectively communicate Christianity in ways that others can grasp. As the late evangelist Paul Little used to say, this is "putting the cookies on the bottom shelf"—that is, making complex and controversial topics accessible through easy-to-remember nuggets of insight and wisdom.

Here's my prediction: when you finish reading *The God Conversation*, you're going to feel better equipped and more motivated to reach out to others with the message of Christ. You'll quickly see for yourself how much God can use illustrations to open minds and warm hearts to the gospel.

Oh, and before you start reading, grab a yellow highlighter. You're going to need it!

Lee Strobel
author, The Case for the Real Jesus

Introduction

It finally happened. For weeks you had prayed for the chance to talk to your coworker about God, and then a door unexpectedly opened. Over lunch, amid talk about work and sports you had it: The God conversation. For thirty minutes you discussed God and how he fits in your life. Your friend asked a few questions but spent most of the time listening.

Now the conversation is over.

Back at your workstation, you are flooded with questions: *What did he think about what I said? Did I make sense? Will he avoid me next time we meet in the cafeteria? What did my friend take away from the conversation?*

The answer to this last question is not encouraging. Research in communication says that when people leave a conversation, they immediately forget half of what was said. Half! And worse than that, eight hours later they will remember only about 20 percent of what was discussed.

What makes up the part they do remember? It's examples.

The illustrations, stories and quotes you sprinkled throughout your conversation will stay with your friend long after the conversation ends. According to communication experts, the most important part of any conversation is when you say, "Think of it this way . . ." or "For example . . ." Illustrations are like calling cards salespeople leave with you after the sales pitch. The calling card you take with you serves as a reminder of the case they made. Every time you come across that salesperson's card, you are reminded of what he or she said. Similarly, every time your friend thinks of the illustrations you used to explain your faith, he or she will remember the point you were making.

The *Wall Street Journal* reports that comedian Bob Hope so treasured his illustrations that he built a walk-in vault with a six-inch-thick steel door to protect file cabinets filled with illustrations, jokes and quotes. Should Bob Hope be the only one to collect and value stories and illustrations? No. Christians, too, need to gather illustrations that will make people think.

Peter tells us that each of us needs to be ready to give an explanation for the hope that is in us (1 Pet 3:15). Today a lot needs to be explained:

- In a world filled with suffering, why doesn't God do more? Doesn't he care about our pain?

- Buddhists, Muslims, Jews and Hindus all have just as much sincerity as Christians. How can Christians claim they alone have a corner on God?

- All of us have the right to choose our own lifestyle, don't we? If it doesn't hurt anyone else, then we have a right to live as we see fit. You can't call others sinners just because they don't see things your way.

The thoughts and questions our friends have about God and the Christian faith require careful answers. Our answers require study of the Scriptures, reading of Christian thinkers and sensitivity to the Holy Spirit. They also require vivid illustrations to make our answers clear and memorable.

The God Conversation provides you with illustrations that will linger with your unbelieving friends, coworkers and family members long after the conversation ends. It gives you rich examples, quotes and stories that will help explain the Christian worldview in your conversations, blogs, e-mails, letters and speeches.

We've been training students, pastors, educators and laypeople in apologetics for a combined total of seventy years and have given apologetic presentations on more than three hundred college campuses. *The God Conversation* is our attempt to share with you some of our favorite illustrations, stories and quotes.

The illustrations you'll read in *The God Conversation* come from current events (terrorist attacks of 9/11, Hurricane Katrina, Mars probe, Bosnian war trials, Virginia Tech shootings), films (*Crash, Catch Me If You Can, Erin Brockovich, The Truman Show*), favorite TV programs (*American Idol, My Name Is Earl, Law & Order, America's Most Wanted*), popular cultural figures (Bono, Oprah, Sharon Stone) and the parables of Jesus. *The God Conversation* also contains some of the most effective illustrations from past and current thinkers, including William Paley, C. S. Lewis, Alvin Plantinga, Machiavelli, Os Guinness, John Stott, Norman Geisler, Alan Dershowitz and Martin Luther King Jr. All the illustrations are short and easy to remember.

HOW THE BOOK IS ORGANIZED

The God Conversation is organized around assumptions your friends have that make accepting the truths of Christianity highly unlikely. For short, philosophers call such assumptions *defeater beliefs*. For example, some of your neighbors may believe that all religions are equally valid ways to God. Because they hold this belief, they believe it can't be true that Christianity is the only way to God. Some of your family members may embrace the belief that it's wrong to judge other people. Consequently, they think your belief that the Scriptures have the authority to morally judge people can't be true. Some of your coworkers may believe that people in Jesus' day were gullible and superstitious and that belief in miracles is a remnant of prescientific cultures. In our scientific age (they believe) you have to be pretty uninformed to still believe in such things.

In this book we lay out what we consider to be the five most likely defeater beliefs you'll encounter as you share your Christian convictions:

1. God can't be good, as seen by all the pain and suffering in the world today (chapters two and three).

2. Christianity can't be the only way to God, because Buddhists, Muslims, Hindus and Jews are just as sincere in their faith as Christians (chapters four and five).

3. The biblical accounts of Jesus rising from the dead can't be trusted, because legend has replaced fact in the disciples' telling of the resurrection (chapters six and seven).

4. You can't judge another person, because there's no ultimate sense of what is right and wrong for everyone (chapters eight and nine).

5. Arguing that God made each of us in his image can't be true because of the fact of evolution (chapters ten and eleven).

As we respond to each of these beliefs, you'll notice some unique features of our book that we hope will make sharing the Christian worldview easier.

First, we've laid out each chapter in a conversational format. The goal of *The God Conversation* is to have you engage in authentic *conversations*, not one-sided lectures. Conversations cannot be scripted. A conversation is like a road trip with many diversions and detours. All true conversations involve a give-and-take process. You present your perspective and the other person responds with a question or objection. In genuine dialogue, questions are not a nuisance but rather are opportunities to engage. In the chapters that follow we've tried to anticipate objections your skeptical friends may have toward the Christian worldview.

Second, we know that in many cases our answers, while substantive, are just touching the tip of the iceberg. Indeed, entire books have been written about each of the issues you'll read about within this one volume. And so each chapter contains Digging Deeper sections that go into more depth concerning a particular question or issue. Also, as we complete our treatment of each major theme, the chapters conclude with our suggestions of other books you can read to supplement ours.

Last, we've broken each chapter into numerous sections. If you think of each chapter as one lengthy, complex conversation, then you'll most likely feel overwhelmed and stop before you begin. The goal is to have multiple conversations spread out over days, weeks or even years when you sprinkle in illustrations that your coworkers or friends will remember and take with them. For easy reading (and quick review), we have set off the stories and illustrations we use with a rule down the side. The answers you'll read in the following pages are packaged in brief, easy-to-read and easy-to-use ways, and we have focused our energies and expertise on helping you communicate these answers to real people in real conversations. It is this last distinctive that sets our book apart from most books on apologetics. If this book gives you fresh insight and new tools for being successful in sharing your faith, we will have succeeded.

Our prayer is that you'll be able to have rich God conversations with those you most care about. In these conversations the illustrations you use, along with the convicting power of the Holy Spirit, will stay with individuals and cause them to wrestle with the truths of Christianity.

1

The Power of Illustrations

An adult bookstore opens for business. Residents of a small southern community are shocked. Two elderly ladies who have lived in the community their entire lives are livid. They complain to the mayor and other town officials in vain. So they take matters into their own hands. Every hour the bookstore is open, one of the ladies stands outside with a camera, taking pictures of anyone who leaves the store. Day after day, embarrassed customers encounter an unexpected photo op. After two months, customers are chased away and the store closes. One of the ladies later confesses that they didn't even have film in the cameras.

I (Tim) read that story more than twenty years ago. I still remember every detail and the point the author was making—it's never too late to get involved in community activism. We wrote this book because we believe that illustrations such as the above are the lifeblood of communication. This conviction is shared by many. Roman philosopher and statesman Seneca stated that "rules make the learner's path long; examples make it short and successful."[1]

PURPOSES OF AN ILLUSTRATION

Why are illustrations so important? We can think of at least four reasons.

First, a good illustration makes the idea you are presenting to your non-Christian friend clear and easy to follow. A well-crafted illustration aids understanding by making an idea more clear through examples that amplify and illustrate the meaning.

We admire individuals who can offer examples and illustrations of what they believe. A friend of ours was discussing the crucial role a person's credentials play in persuading us. He was speaking in fairly theoretical terms until one person in the group asked for an example.

He told them about a communication expert who tried an experiment on fellow health club members. This expert approached people in the club and asked if they had heard of the latest diet craze. The diet had been completely fabricated by him and was based on his love of chocolate. But he told club members that the creators of the diet claimed that if overweight people, in addition to eating a normal diet and exercising moderately, were to eat three chocolate éclairs a day, they would lose weight. He said it had been discovered that chocolate éclairs contain a special nutrient—encomial dioxin—that attacks calories.

"You've got to be kidding!" was the common response.

Ignoring their rolled eyes, the expert told the health club members that the diet had been tested and had full support from experts at Johns Hopkins. Upon hearing the name of Johns Hopkins, people paused and began asking questions about the diet. Based on the credibility of a prestigious university, the absurd seemed plausible.

The people in the group laughed at our friend's story but got the point. We find the credibility of well-known institutions to be very persuasive.

Providing this type of clarity is crucial when you are sharing arguments for God's existence or the uniqueness of Christianity with your unbelieving friends. Not only will the illustrations in this book help you understand arguments for God's existence or the uniqueness of Christ; they will help your unbelieving neighbor or coworker understand as well. Some of the arguments in *The God Conversation* may be new to you. Our hope is that the illustrations in this book will help you and your friends understand the arguments more clearly.

Second, the purpose of an illustration is to help your friend remember the point you are making. When the conversation is over, your friend will take with him or her the illustrations you used. Jesus knew this and utilized the power of illustrations. Memorable words were especially important in biblical times, when people in the marketplace weren't exactly taking notes on their laptop computers or BlackBerrys.

The next time you read through the Gospels, pay attention to how Jesus illustrates his ideas. The lamp under the bushel (Lk 8:16), the city on top of a hill (Mt 5:14), the Good Samaritan (Lk 10:25-37) and the camel and the eye of the needle (Mk 10:25) are enduring illustrations. Two thousand years later we still remember and use Jesus' vivid examples.

It's easy to forget an idea, but stories have a lingering effect. The more we sprinkle our conversations with well-crafted illustrations and examples, the more memorable our conversations will be.

Third, a good illustration allows repetition without weariness. No one likes to be lectured to. Any parent knows that children will quickly become fidgety during lengthy parental speeches. Yet if you tell them a story about *you* growing up and how *you* encountered similar challenges, your children will be more apt to pay attention. You will be making the same point as in the speech, but it will be repackaged.

The same principle is true for apologetic conversations. For example, in our chapter discussing the argument from design (chapter ten), we state that the argument is based on three key ideas:

1. Where there is design, there is a designer.

2. Signs of design are obvious in our bodies and in the world around us.

3. The design we see in ourselves and in the world should be attributed to an intelligent Designer.

Makes sense, doesn't it? But you can state these three ideas only so many times in a conversation before your friend feels browbeaten.

Instead of merely repeating the three ideas, share with your listener William Paley's illustration comparing the human eye to a high-powered telescope. In this illustration Paley observes that both the eye and the telescope are carefully designed to reflect rays of light and bring objects into focus. He concludes that if we attribute the design of the telescope to a master craftsman, then surely we ought also to attribute the design of the human eye to a divine craftsman. What has Paley just said? The same three points listed above.

What Paley's illustration accomplishes is what educators cleverly refer to as *creative redundancy*. The same content is shared in a different package.

Finally, a good illustration sustains the interest of the listener. In his lectures on preaching, R. W. Dale states that "monotony is almost always fatal to interest; monotony of voice, monotony of style, monotony of intellectual activity."[2] He's right, isn't he? Many of our apologetic arguments, if we are not careful, can be overloaded with facts. If we tell our friend that we have five reasons for believing Jesus is God, he or she may lose interest after the first or second point. Illustrations are a way to reclaim the interest of our friends. A well-crafted illustra-

tion can also bring a person into the conversation as an active participant. That's why many of the illustrations we've included in this book
are compelling situations that invite the listener to respond to a real
or imaginary story or circumstance.

For example, in the next chapter many of the illustrations you'll read
will ask your skeptical friend to view life from God's perspective. If your
friend was God, what would he or she do to stop the evil in our world?
Set a deadline of some sort? Once it was set, how would your friend en-
force the deadline? As God, would your friend zap a would-be terrorist
with high-voltage electricity to keep him from blowing up an airplane?
Perhaps evil could be eliminated by converting all humans into mindless puppets? Such illustrations turn your coworker from being a pas-
sive partner in a conversation to being active and involved.

MAKING THIS BOOK EFFECTIVE

Just as a public speaker runs through his or her speech multiple times,
so we encourage you as the reader of *The God Conversation* to practice.
Most of the quotes listed in the chapters are short and can be easily
memorized, such as Voltaire's thought-provoking idea found in chapter eleven: "If a watch proves the existence of a watchmaker but the
universe does not prove the existence of a great architect, then I consent to be called a fool." The illustrations in this book have been carefully written and edited so they can be committed to memory and
then put into the reader's own words. You will be introduced to examples of how key illustrations, such as Paley's famous watch illustration, can be paraphrased without losing the power of his argument. As
a result, readers of *The God Conversation* will come away with a store-
house of resources to use during any conversation.

The first collection of illustrations you'll read focus on the most
pressing issue of our post-9/11 culture: Is God still good in a world of
evil?

2

Can God Be Good If Terrorists Exist?

When you think about suffering, what images come to mind? Sadly, there are plenty to choose from. The sight of thick black smoke pouring out of twin skyscrapers on September 11. A massive wave in Asia that pummels eleven countries, leaving tens of thousands dead. A roadside bomb exploding while American soldiers hand out toys to Iraqi children on Christmas day. Thirty-three students killed by a deranged shooter on Virginia Tech's campus. Or perhaps your image is more personal. A family member or friend who suffers through a long illness.

With these images come questions: Is God immune to our suffering? Why did he allow evil to enter our world in the first place? Where was he on 9/11? Why doesn't he just put an end to pain and suffering? Questions like these foster responses ranging from puzzlement to despair to anger. "The only thing you can say about God," quips Woody Allen, "is that he's an underachiever."

While answers are hard to come by, one thing is clear—we live in a world filled with pain. Yet as Christians we believe that God is good, aware of our pain and committed to us. How can these beliefs be reconciled?

In a media-saturated world where disasters, sickness and acts of terrorism are graphically displayed on television and the Internet, Christians need to be ready to explain to others how a good God can exist in a world of turmoil.

THINKING ABOUT EVIL

Perhaps more than any other issue, the problem of evil raises powerful emotions and sparks unanswered questions. When people's lives are touched by suffering, they tend not to experience just one emotion but a rush of emotions such as sadness, bitterness, confusion, despair and anger. Theologian Cornelius Plantinga Jr. describes the toll these emotions can take on a person:

> A woman came out of a sickroom where a loved one was dying and asked in a tightly controlled voice, "Is there a room anywhere in the hospital where I can go and scream?" A doctor directed her to a place and later mused over the idea that every hospital—maybe every office and home—ought to have a screaming room.[1]

He's right, isn't he?

Anyone might want to scream in the face of tragedy. When discussing the problem of evil with those outside the Christian community, it's important to make clear that we *all* wrestle with this issue, regardless of our view of God. Individuals become defensive when their personal thoughts, experiences and questions are met with distant neutrality. However, when we meet their views with empathy and acknowledgment of hurts or struggles, they feel valued. So let the people you're speaking with know that Christians are not neutral or detached when it comes to suffering. We have the same urge to visit a screaming room as they do.

Rather than jumping into a quick reply to questions concerning God and evil, consider starting with an illustration that acknowledges people's emotions. Let them know that the questions and emotions they wrestle with were shared by one of Christianity's greatest defenders: C. S. Lewis.

C. S. LEWIS IN THE SCREAMING ROOM

When Lewis's wife, Joy Gresham, died of cancer, he was devastated. In *A Grief Observed* Lewis lets us in on the anger and confusion he experienced after his loss: "Where is God? . . . Go to Him when your need is desperate, when all other help is in vain, and what do you find? A door slammed in your face, and a sound of bolting and double bolting on the inside. After that silence. You may as well turn away."[2]

Lewis is candid in saying that he could have used a screaming room of his own. In fact, after Joy's much-prayed-for remission ends, he did yell at God. "Time after time," Lewis wrote, "when He seemed most gracious, He was preparing the next torture. . . . I wrote that last night. It was a yell rather than a thought."[3]

After recounting Lewis's struggles, ask if your friend can relate to his feelings. Does he feel betrayed by God? Does suffering cause her to want to yell at God? What questions does suffering bring up?

Acknowledging people's feelings is not difficult. First, it means letting them know that you are attempting to understand the significance of their questions and emotions. Second, it means communicating that their feelings are important to you and that you struggle with some of the same doubts and feelings. "It is in suffering," suggests one theologian, "that the whole human question about God arises."[4] To be human is to wrestle with the reality of evil.

After communicating that both Christians and non-Christians wrestle with the problem of evil, be prepared to respond to some poignant questions that those touched by suffering ask. The following questions, though numbered, are not presented in any particular order. Why? Because when people wrestle with evil, they are often flooded with questions that overlap and even contradict each other. In this chapter and the next we'll consider seven troubling questions. As you read our responses, remember that each question will most likely be a separate conversation that could be spaced out over days or weeks.

QUESTION 1: WHY DID GOD ALLOW THE POSSIBILITY OF EVIL AND SUFFERING?

In light of the greatest act of terrorism against the United States (September 11, 2001), the greatest natural disaster to hit our shores (Hurricane Katrina) and the deadliest shooting on an American college campus (Virginia Tech), this question makes sense. If God exists, then why didn't he create a world free of terrorism and hurricanes? To answer this question adequately, we must consider God's perspective.

Central to effective communication is the ability to engage in perspective-taking with another person. Perspective-taking is the ability to assume another person's point of view and see the world through his or her eyes. The choices individuals make will make sense to us only if we understand how they view particular situations and the choices available to them. The same is true with God. To understand the world God created, we need to know the choices available to him.[5] Would God create a world of robots that would never disobey him or create human beings who could? Christian philosopher Norman Geisler puts it this way: "To be free we had to have not only the opportunity to choose good, but also the ability to choose evil. That was the risk God knowingly took."[6]

The following illustration helps us understand why God chose humans over robots.

MR. WONDERFUL DOLL AND FREE CHOICE

One of the hottest gifts today for female shoppers is the Mr. Wonderful Doll. He's twelve inches tall, handsome and (most important to women) sensitive. This perfect man is programmed to always say the right thing. Simply push a button to hear him say one of sixteen phrases:

"You take the remote. As long as I'm with you, I don't care what we watch."

"The ball game is not that important. I'd rather spend time with you."

"Why don't we go to the mall? Didn't you want some shoes?"

"You know, I think it's really important to talk about our relationship."

"You've been on my mind all day. That's why I bought you these flowers."

The best thing about Mr. Wonderful is that he never disappoints! He's never irritable, sarcastic or selfish. So long as you keep putting in three AA batteries, he'll continue to affirm and compliment whoever is pushing his button. For those of us who are married, it's certainly understandable why such a doll would be desirable.

God could have done the same. That is, he could have created a world of Wonderful Human Dolls. Each time God pressed our button, we'd be programmed to say:

"God, you have been on my mind all day."

"So long as I'm with you, God, I don't care what we do."

DIGGING DEEPER

The fact that a good and all-pow-erful God doesn't rid the world of all evil has often been used by atheists to suggest that a belief in God entails an unavoidable contradiction. Atheists used to argue that, given evil, God could not exist, because the following three sentences are contradic-tory: (1) God is all-powerful. (2) God is all-loving. (3) Evil exists. According to atheist thinkers, if God is all-powerful and all-lov-ing, he would want to do away with evil and he would be power-ful enough to do so, and there-fore evil would not exist. But this contradicts the fact that evil does exist.

We mentioned that atheists used to use this argument, but they do not use it any longer, be-cause this problem of evil has been solved. The solution is pretty obvious: God could have good reasons, perhaps known only to himself, for permitting evil. If this were the case, God could still exist along with evil.

"God, you are holy, perfect and wor-thy of my love."

"God, I would never disobey you."

In a world of human dolls there would be no evil. Why? Because lying, cheating, rape, murder, abuse, racism and sexism would not be part of our programming. All we would do, like the Mr. Wonderful Doll, would be to con-tinually fawn over God. It would be a perfect world, free of evil.

But would a relationship with a doll really satisfy?

At this point in the conversation, ask the person with whom you're speaking if he or she could think of any draw-backs to having a relationship with a Mr. or Mrs. Wonderful Doll. Take time to list the negatives of such a relation-ship. For example, while Mr. Wonderful can say, "I love you," does he mean it? Would mindless compliments be enough?

The atheist thinker Jean-Paul Sartre didn't think such programmed re-sponses would be meaningful. He wrote, "The man who wants to be loved does not desire the enslavement of the beloved. He is not bent on becoming the object of passion which flows forth mechanically. He does not want to possess an automaton."[7] For Sartre, to know that your lover has been programmed to love you cheapens the love.

God agrees.

God paid the human race the greatest compliment we could receive—he didn't program us to mechanically love him. The decision not to make us love God is graphically seen when Jesus stands on the outskirts of Jerusalem, the symbol of Jewish pride, and says, "Jerusalem, Jerusalem . . . how often I have longed to gather your children together, as a hen gathers her chicks." Jesus summarizes the people's response to him in four tragic words: "You were not willing" (Mt 23:37). Like the people of Jerusalem, we can either cultivate a relationship with God or resist his invitation. Unfortunately, we have chosen to spurn his offer. As a result, we created a world of pain and evil.

QUESTION 2: WITH SO MUCH EVIL IN THE WORLD TODAY, WHY DOESN'T GOD JUST STOP IT?

When people ask this question, they usually have some specific instance of evil in mind. This is the type of question a person asks after hearing of a terrorist attack or learning that a loved one has taken ill.

Before answering this question, it would be wise to discover the personal history behind the question. The writer of Proverbs reminds us that the "purposes of a man's heart are deep waters" (Prov 20:5). The job of a good conversationalist is to "draw them out" (to use the words of that same proverb). Before you begin to answer, take time to draw out what is prompting this question.

When you do respond, paint a picture for your listener of what it would look like if God did exactly what she is asking him to do—stop *all* evil.

GOD SETS A DEADLINE

What if God took the radical step of setting a deadline for ridding the world of evil?[8] Suppose God announces that next Monday at midnight he will step in and stop all suffering caused by evil people. How would he do that? Let's say God decides to use a tool carried by many police officers—a Taser gun.

A Taser gun shoots an individual with a temporary, high-voltage current of electricity. The makers of Taser guns claim that a shock lasting half a second will cause intense pain and muscle contraction. Two to three seconds will cause a person to become dazed and drop to the ground. Anything longer than three seconds will drop an attacker for up to fifteen minutes. The makers of Taser guns boast of a 95 percent compliance rate. In other words, hit a person with enough electricity and you can get him to do anything.

When the deadline for stopping evil comes, God gets us to comply with his wishes by shocking us. Start to tell a lie and you are hit with a half-second zap. Try to rob a person and you get two seconds of shock. A would-be murderer would be incapacitated. However, knowing that evil thoughts often lead to evil actions, God also zaps us for sinister thoughts. But God's still not finished. Since it's evil to fail to do good when given the opportunity, God zaps us for failing to show mercy, kindness and justice. As a result, people are zapped for doing evil acts, thinking evil thoughts and failing to do what is right.

What would be the result? A world of twitchy people, who obey God like a cowering, beaten dog.

After sharing this illustration, ask your listener what might be a drawback to such an approach.

One possible drawback is that individuals would be morally good for fear of being shocked. God would stop the action, but a person's heart would be unaffected. People who write on parenting make a distinction between deep acting and surface acting. Surface acting involves controlling a child's outward expression of emotions, not influencing what the child actually feels. Expressing respect is emphasized more than being respectful. In contrast, deep acting seeks to affect a child's heart and attitude. Children should be respectful of adults because that is the right thing to do. If God shocked people every time they did evil, he would get a world of surface actors—people acting virtuously while harboring ill feelings toward others and God. "It is worth noting that the whole point of Christianity," explains J. B. Phillips, "lies not in interference with the human power to choose, but in producing a willing consent to choose good rather than evil."[9]

Another reason God doesn't set a deadline for ending evil is that evil forces us to come face-to-face with the world we've created. Evil and pain prod us to think about the kind of world God desires for us—a world free of violence, destruction and suffering. This line of thinking is powerfully articulated by C. S. Lewis: "God whispers to us in our pleasures, speaks in our conscience, but shouts in our pains: it is His megaphone to rouse a deaf world."[10] God allows evil to continue because it forces us to ask the *why* questions.

GOD'S MEGAPHONE—THIS ISN'T RIGHT!

In the sixth season of *American Idol* producers launch a campaign called *Idol Gives Back*. The campaign is designed to address poverty in the USA and Africa through viewer donations. To drum up support America's favorite caustic critic, Simon Cowell, travels to an African village ravished by poverty and disease. During one stop he goes into a small shack that houses a mother and fourteen children (eight of them AIDS orphans she's taken in). A visibly shaken Cowell looks in the camera and confesses: "I didn't know this existed." The camera crew follows him as he moves among malnourished, sickly villagers, saying, "This isn't right! This isn't right!"

GOD'S MEGAPHONE—WHERE DID EVIL COME FROM?

During World War II, on the island of Guadalcanal, the Japanese were building an airbase to strike American ships. On August 7, 1942, some 10,000 Marines went ashore to capture the airfield. They were met with fierce resistance from the Japanese, who often attacked at night in suicide charges. In six months 1,752 Americans died and a staggering 24,000 Japanese perished in a futile attempt to turn back the invasion. In the movie *A Thin Red Line,* an American soldier views the human carnage after one night attack. He reflects: "Where did evil come from? How did it steal its way into the world, mocking us for what could have been?"

DIGGING DEEPER

Another reason God doesn't just stop evil is because evil is not a thing that can be disposed of like a bag of garbage. Evil is a lack of what should be the case. Evil is when things aren't the way they are supposed to be. When the hard drive of a computer crashes, it is dysfunctional; it isn't operating the way it was designed to function. Whatever is causing the hard drive to crash can be seen as a type of evil. Thinking of evil this way presupposes that there is a Designer who makes things to function a certain way. When they don't, evil exists.

When God uses evil as a megaphone to rouse us, it accomplishes two things.

First, similar to Simon Cowell's reaction, suffering *forces* us to acknowledge that something "isn't right" in our troubled world. If Cowell, a multi-millionaire obsessed with finding America's next pop star, can't avoid the reality and implications of evil, how can we? Most importantly, evil forces us to wrestle with the question that haunted the American soldier: "Where did evil come from?"

Second, when God shouts to us through suffering and pain, it has a haunting effect. "It's much harder to believe the world is here just so I can party," writes Philip Yancey, "when a third of its people go to bed starving each night. It's much harder to believe the purpose of life is to feel good when I see teenagers smashed on a freeway. If I try to escape the idea and merely enjoy life, suffering is there, haunting me."[11] As Christians we, too, are haunted by suffering and the deep questions associated with evil. Illustrations such as these open the door to discuss how we can fix our world—an issue central to the Christian worldview.

QUESTION 3: IS GOD IMMUNE TO OUR SUFFERING?

How does God feel when he watches a hijacked plane filled with frightened passengers slam into a building? Does the pain in our world bother him? Most important, can he empathize with our grief? When answering these questions, it's useful to first define empathy and then show how God moves beyond empathy.

Empathy is the ability to project oneself into the perspective of another to imagine, feel and understand how that person views and experiences the world. The ability to imagine the struggles, pains and perspective of another person is a crucial relational skill.

FATHER DAMIEN MOVES BEYOND EMPATHY

Father Damien, at his own request, was assigned to a leper colony on Molokai Island, Hawaii, in 1873. The colony had no medical doctor or priest to care for them. Father Damien's motivation for going was simple—he couldn't imagine a person living out his or her last days in isolation with no one to care for that person. With profound empathy, Father Damien did everything for the members of the colony—he bathed them, dressed festering ulcers, built coffins, dug graves and held worship services. He served the colony for twelve years.

One Sunday everything changed. Father Damien stood in front of the congregation of lepers and opened his robes to show the first signs of leprosy. He began his sermon with the words "We lepers."[12]

After sharing this illustration, introduce two questions into the conversation.

First, how did the lepers' view of Father Damien change after his announcement? Before the priest contracted leprosy, the inhabitants of the colony no doubt viewed him as an empathetic outsider trying to understand and evaluate the plight of lepers. He was a healthy man attempting to imagine the horrors of leprosy. After the announcement, their view of him was irrevocably changed. He was now one of them—a leper.

The second question focuses on God's relation to us—is God's understanding of our suffering more similar to the perspective of Father Damien *before* he contracted leprosy or *after*? In other words, is God an outsider trying to empathize with our suffering or an insider who has personally experienced our pain? Christianity's radical answer is that God does not merely empathize with our suffering; he has experienced it firsthand.

Christians believe that God put on human flesh and suffered many of the evils that plague us. The prophet Isaiah informed listeners that the coming Messiah would be "a man of sorrows, and familiar with suffering" (Is 53:3). Even a casual reading of the Gospels show that Isaiah's prophecy came true. In his short life Christ experienced hunger, pain, abandonment, injustice, beatings and discouragement. This belief—that God has suffered—sets Christianity apart from other religions. "The chief difference between Christianity and other theistic religions," suggests Christian philosopher Alvin Plantinga, "lies just here: according to the Christian Gospel, God is willing to enter into and share the sufferings of his creatures, in order to redeem them and his world."[13] Because Jesus has shared in our sufferings, we can be assured that he sympathizes with us as we negotiate a world filled with pain (Heb 4:14-16).

The fact that God has suffered has a powerful silencing effect on those who claim he is indifferent or immune to our suffering.

THE SUFFERING JUDGE

William Lane Craig tells the story of three men standing before God's throne on Judgment Day.

> Each had a score to settle with God. "I was hanged for a crime I didn't commit," complained one man bitterly. "I died from a disease that dragged on for months, leaving me broken in both body and spirit," said another. "My son was killed in the prime of his life when a drunk behind the wheel jumped the curb and ran him down," muttered the third. Each was angry and anxious to give God a piece of his mind. But when they reached the throne and saw their Judge with His nail-scarred hands and feet and His wounded side, a "man of sorrows and acquainted with grief," each mouth was stopped.[14]

What silenced these three individuals? Each came face-to-face with a God who suffered the sort of injustice, physical suffering and tragedy they angrily described. Christ was an innocent man unjustly sentenced to a brutal death. His body was broken by whippings and beatings, and his spirit was tormented when God turned away during the crucifixion. Three years into his public ministry, while in his prime, his life came to a violent end.

Whatever conclusion a person comes to concerning the problem of pain, one fact is clear—God does not need to project himself into our pain. He experienced it.

Can God Be Good If Terrorists Exist?
(Part 2)

When FEMA official Marty Bahamonde viewed the destruction of Hurricane Katrina, he was overwhelmed by the human suffering. What haunted him most were the faces of children. He wrote in an e-mail, "I can't get out of my head the visions of the children and babies I saw sitting there, helpless, looking at me and hoping I could make a difference."[1]

Like this FEMA official, all of us were haunted by the stories of suffering that came out of Hurricane Katrina. Tragedies such as these provoke powerful questions: Is God to blame for hurricanes and tsunamis? How does God respond to the death of children? Why doesn't God do more? Most important, can I still trust him in the presence of evil?

QUESTION 4: WHO'S TO BLAME FOR HURRICANES, TSUNAMIS AND CANCER?

When things go wrong, we are quick to assign blame. It makes sense to most people that evils such as murder, rape and robbery are human evils and that we bear the responsibility. Yet who should bear the responsibility for floods, hurricanes or cancer? When insurance adjusters evaluate the devastation caused by a flood, they refer to it as an "act of God." Shouldn't God shoulder the responsibility for natural evils?

When asked if God should be blamed for the reality of natural disasters, our response is no. Christians believe that humans were given the responsibility of being caretakers for earth. When the first humans—Adam and Eve—rebelled against God, two results followed. First, when we turned away from him, God judged not only us but creation as well. The Scriptures state that our world was "subjected to frustration" and longs to be released (Rom 8:20-22). One sign of this futility is the vulnerability to disease and natural disasters we see today. Second, the more we neglect our responsibility as caretakers of the earth, the more the earth declines. Our actions directly affect the planet we live on.

As you offer this answer, be aware that this may be the first time a person has heard such a perspective. The movie *Erin Brockovich* depicts how our actions influence our surroundings.

POISONED WATER—WHO'S TO BLAME?

The residents of Hinkley, California, helplessly watch their children, spouses and pets get sick and even die. They are frantic to find the cause. Ironically, the one thing that no one suspects is the culprit— the water. With every glass of water the townspeople drink, they ingest poison. For years a major corporation has dumped toxic materials into a faulty water well, which has slowly poisoned the town's drinking supply. Through a bitter court case, spearheaded by Erin Brockovich (played by Julia Roberts), it's discovered that the corporation failed to safely dispose of toxic materials. Fueled by greed, they set aside their civic and legal responsibility to care for the environment. Community members live in a toxic environment created by corporate greed, self-interest and deceit.

The same is true of our spoiled world. By putting our own interests in front of our responsibility to follow God and care for the world, we have made the world a dangerous place. The earth was poisoned by our rebellion. Tornadoes, hurricanes, cancer and similar tragedies are constant reminders of our turn from God. These natural disasters are also evidence that our God-given job to be caretakers of the earth is real and that abandoning that job has real ramifications.

When discussing natural evils, it's important to note that many evils are made worse by our action or inaction.

RACISM AND AFRICAN AID

In a Rolling Stone interview, Bono—AIDS activist and lead singer of U2—reveals how discouraging it is to find that what keeps many from responding to the plight of African children is a sense of racial superiority.

> A prominent head of state said to me if we really believed that these people in the developing world were equal, there is no way that we could allow 3,000 Africans, mostly children, to die every day from mosquito bites while we have the medicines and technology that could save their lives. It's as absurd as separate drinking fountains for blacks in the 1950s. It's racism disguised by distance.[2]

At this point in the conversation, ask the person with whom you're speaking what the world would look like if we set aside political differences or racism and marshaled the world's resources to deal with the plight of Africa. For instance, after hearing that a mosquito net costs only $15 and could protect a family from malaria for five years, actress Sharon Stone stood up at a meeting and pledged $10,000 toward mosquito nets. She implored the audience to give as well. In five minutes she raised $1 million. The effects on our spoiled world would be greatly reduced if we set aside sinful attitudes and cared for others and the earth as God commands.

DIGGING DEEPER

Ironically, there can be a problem of evil only if there is a God. Theists may have a problem of evil, but atheists have a problem of goodness—how could there be goodness in a godless universe? If there is no God, the only answer to "Why did that earthquake kill 30,000 people?" is "Why not?" We would have no reason to think that things like this shouldn't happen. The occurrence of evil would no longer be strange. In a godless universe, stuff happens and that's the end of the matter.

QUESTION 5: WHAT ABOUT THE SUFFERING OF CHILDREN?

The atheist thinker Bertrand Russell argued that no one could sit at the bedside of dying child and maintain a belief in God. While the death of any child is heart-wrenching, it's important to understand how God reacts to such a tragedy.

Some theologians believe that when a child dies, he or she is immediately ushered into God's presence to experience his love and care. In God's sight children who die before reaching an "age of responsibility" are not yet culpable for wrong actions and therefore are judged morally innocent. "If a child dies before he or she is capable of making genuine moral decisions," suggests theologian Millard Erickson, "there is only innocence."[3] Erickson's conclusion finds support from Robert Lightner, who argues that Jesus does not seem to regard chil-

DIGGING DEEPER

God judged the creation as a result of the fall of angels and humans such that disease and natural disasters now occur. He did this for two reasons. First, we were put here to be stewards of the earth. If it were the case that no ill effects came about when that stewardship was abused, then we would not really be stewards. Because our stewardship is real, the creation was subjected to frustration when the fall occurred. Second, natural disasters are warning signs that something deeply troubling is wrong with this world and that this is not our real home.

dren as fundamentally sinful, at least in their willful rejection of God, and points to them as an example of the simple trust and utter dependence necessary to enter the kingdom of heaven (Mt 18:3; 19:14).[4]

John MacArthur, after citing notable theologians such as B. B. Warfield and C. H. Spurgeon, writes, "Little children are called innocent in Scripture for precisely this reason: They have no willful rebellion against God. They have no deeds of disbelief." MacArthur acknowledges that while all children are born with a sinful nature, "they have never had willful opportunity to exercise that nature with full understanding or deliberate rebellion."[5]

A perspective we find particularly compelling is Millard Erickson's argument gleaned from Romans 5. Erickson points to the parallelism in Romans 5, where Adam's sin and Christ's righteousness are applied to us. Adam's sin leads to death, while Christ's righteousness leads to eternal life (Rom 5:18). What does this parallel show us? "If, as we might be inclined to think, the condemnation and guilt of Adam are imputed to us without there being on our part any sort of conscious choice of his act, the same would necessarily be true of the imputation of Christ's redeeming work."[6] In other words, if we say that Adam's sin is immediately applied to us at birth, then we must say the same about Christ's righteousness. However, we know that isn't the case. Paul states that the righteousness of Christ is applied to an individual only after he or she makes a conscious decision to receive the "abundant provision of grace" and the "gift of righteousness" God offers through Christ (Rom 5:17). Erickson argues that, similar to Christ's righteousness, Adam's sin is applied only after a "conscious and voluntary decision on our part."

What would this decision look like in the life of a child? Adam's sin is *not* applied to a child the first time he or she sins. Rather, it is applied when a child realizes he or she has a bent toward sinning. "We become responsible and guilty when we accept or approve of our corrupt nature. There is a time in the life of each one of us when we become aware of our own tendency toward sin."[7]

THE AGE OF ACCOUNTABILITY AND DINNER DECORUM

You spend all day cooking. The smells coming out of the kitchen are unbelievable. You help your children set the table. After each plate is filled to capacity, you all dive in. After one mouthful, your five-year-old son looks at you and says, "This food tastes like crap!" You could hear a pin drop. He had heard the word "crap" at school and decided to try it out at the dinner table.

After recovering from the shock, you have a decision to make. Does he understand how offensive that word is? Is he deliberately rebelling against dinner time rules you have established and intentionally insulting the adult who made the meal? Or is he a child acting childishly? If he was twelve and regularly used that word to assess your cooking, despite knowing it was wrong, he would be held accountable and would have to accept the consequences. But as a five-year-old, is he responsible?

The same moral distinction you made with your son is what God does perfectly in the case of each child who comes into his presence after a tragedy. Thus many children who come into his presence after a flood, hurricane or wrongdoing are judged innocent and experience his love for eternity.

DIGGING DEEPER

Some argue that the death of a child is a senseless tragedy that is gratuitous—evil that is absurd and without justification. Two things can be said in response to this. First, due to our limited perspective, we are never in a position to say that some evil is gratuitous. Consider a disaster such as a massive earthquake. To judge that it was a pointless evil, we would have to know two sorts of facts: the long-range balance of good versus evil that resulted over centuries from the event happening, and the long-range balance of good versus evil that would have resulted if the event had not happened. Only then could we judge that the event was really gratuitous. But who has the slightest idea of how to make such judgments? Only God has access to the facts that allow him to determine whether an act of evil is gratuitous.

This illustration is not meant to minimize the grief God feels when a child dies. Even though Jesus knew that he would soon raise his friend Lazarus from the dead, he still wept at the reality of death (Jn 11:14-46). The same emotions Christ exhibited at the death of Lazarus are what God feels when any child dies. Even though he knows the child will immediately be with him, God still grieves his or her tragic death.

QUESTION 6: WHY DOESN'T GOD DO MORE?

Three teenagers grab baseball bats, jump into a car and go looking for fun. When they see a homeless man sleeping on a bench, they beat him repeatedly, ignoring his cries to stop. The attack is captured on a surveillance video. The scene is heart wrenching to watch. Yet why didn't God do something? How could he let this happen?

Although watching the video of this brutality evokes powerful emotions, a few thoughts need to be kept in mind. First, Christ himself knows what it's like to be an innocent man beaten by evil men. He is not immune to this man's suffering. Second,

God doesn't force us to be moral. This man was beaten by teens choosing to engage in evil. Last, though God did not stop the beating, we can be assured that he will redeem this man's suffering.

What would the redeeming of this man's pain look like?

This is a true story. And so, while it's impossible to know all the details behind God's redeeming of this situation, we have a few clues. Due to a strategically placed video camera, the three teens have been caught and now stand trial. This beating, though tragic, brought national attention to the plight of the homeless. "This will shine a very bright light on an issue that has been camouflaged and buried for a long time," states an activist in helping the homeless. "People put blinders on until it's right under their nose."[8] This incident indeed sparked a national discussion of how we view the homeless and what should be done to assist them.

God's redeeming of evil is not limited to this one case. Consider the following illustrations.

REDEEMING EVIL—MADD

MADD (Mothers Against Drunk Drivers) is one of the most respected and effective nonprofit organizations in the United States. With more than six hundred chapters, MADD has successfully lobbied for legislation targeting drunk drivers and supporting victim's rights. The group has prevented thousands of deaths. MADD was founded by Cindy Lightner after her thirteen-year-old daughter was killed by a drunk driver as she walked to a school carnival. The driver had three previous convictions for drunk driving. Lawmakers agree that our roads are safer due to revamped drunk driving laws spurred on by Lightner's activism.

REDEEMING EVIL—AMERICA'S MOST WANTED

John Walsh is a tireless advocate for missing children. He has testified before Congress on behalf of parents of missing children and was instrumental in the passing of the Missing Children Act in 1982. His nationally syndicated show *America's Most Wanted* has converted ordinary citizens into crime watchers and has been instrumental in bringing over 900 fugitives to justice. Walsh's activism is fueled by the memory of his son's abduction from a shopping mall in 1981. His son's body was found sixteen days later. Walsh's work has transformed how law enforcement agencies track and recover missing children.

Sharing the above illustrations with those wrestling with the problem of evil isn't meant to minimize the beating of a homeless person, the death of teenage girl or the tragedy of missing children. It's meant to communicate that God is aware of all instances of evil in our world and is actively committed to redeeming the effects of evil. While we cannot always see how God specifically redeems evil in our world, we can know that through the cross of Christ, God does redeem all suffering experienced by his followers.

QUESTION 7: IN THE MIDST OF SO MUCH SUFFERING, CAN I STILL TRUST GOD?

When Billy Graham addressed the families of victims after the Oklahoma City bombing, he spoke about how tragedy affects people differently. For some, suffering provokes profound anger at God. "I trusted you and this happened!" Others, while in midst of grief, still cling to God. The trust somehow holds. Graham prayed for both sets of people: "I pray that you will not let bitterness and poison creep into your souls, but you will turn in faith and trust in God even if we cannot understand. It is better to face something like this with God than without Him."[9]

The reason many retain faith in God while in the midst of suffering is that they have a history with God. Over the years they've experienced God's goodness and have come to trust him. While instances of evil challenge a believer's trust in God, they don't wipe out faith. Somehow, based on what they know about God, individuals still believe the best of him.

BELIEVING THE BEST

C. Stephen Evans's wife leaves him alone to do some quick shopping. She promises that she'll be back in a few minutes to nurse their infant daughter. A few minutes turn into three hours and the baby is hungry. As Evans paces the house with a crying baby, he constantly looks at the clock. Where is she? He's tempted to believe the worst—perhaps she ran into an old friend or went on a shopping spree!

While Evans is distressed and worried, he continues to believe the best about his wife. He explains: "I know the kind of person she is. I know she is not the kind of person to go dancing at a singles bar and leave me alone with the children. She loves me, she cares about me, and she lives up to her commitments. Therefore, if she is later than she promised, she has a good reason."[10]

The reason Christians stay connected to God during times of suffering is that, as with Evans's knowledge of his wife, we are convinced that God loves us and is committed to us.

At this point in the conversation, a person may ask, "How do you know that about God?"

The answer is that, in addition to our having personally experienced the goodness of God, the Scriptures tell us exactly how God feels about evil. How does God feel about death, for instance? The Scriptures state that he does not take pleasure in the death of anyone, even the wicked (Ezek 33:11).

When the whole human race turned its back on God and turned the world into a place of unbearable suffering, God was heartbroken. In an amazing statement the Scriptures say that God's "heart was filled with pain" (Gen 6:6). "Behind that one statement," writes Philip Yancey, "stands all the shock and grief of God as a parent."[11] Yet God did not experience the rebellion of just one child but of a whole race of rebellious children. His allowing himself to be moved by a world enveloped in evil tells us much about the heart of God.

Christian philosopher Alvin Plantinga believes that those who say God cannot suffer are wrong. "God's capacity for suffering," he writes, "is proportional to his greatness; it exceeds our capacity for suffering in the same measure as his capacity for knowledge exceeds ours."[12]

Most important, the Scriptures show us God in action. When God stepped into our world through the person of Christ, he strove against evil. When Christ encountered the hungry, he fed them (Mk 6:34-44; 8:1-8). When he witnessed injustice, he took action (Mk 3:1-6; 11:15-19). He didn't avoid the poor and oppressed; he sought them out (Mt 9:1-8; Mk 5:1-16).

On one occasion a man infected with leprosy—a disease then carrying the same kind of social stigma often associated today with AIDS—approached Christ and asked to be healed (Mt 8:1-4). Christ not only healed him but also, to the astonishment of the crowd, *touched* him. In that one action this individual was healed physically and emotionally. While Christ may not always physically heal us, the same love, care and commitment he showed that suffering man are available to all who pursue him. This love is what Christians cling to in times of suffering.

Whenever we share the illustration of C. Stephen Evans waiting for his wife, people want to know what happened to his wife. Did she ever return? Why was she late? Evans wisely never answers the question. To Evans it doesn't matter why she is late. He trusts her.

In this life we are left waiting like Evans. As we wait we often wonder why God doesn't show up in the manner and at the time we desire. We, like Evans waiting for his wife, must trust in the goodness of God as we wait to be reunited with him.

CONCLUSION

We close this chapter with an illustration of how the love of God, while not fully answering the problem of evil, can be enough to help us cope with evil while in the screaming room.

SEE THEM ON THE OTHER SIDE

In Sago, West Virginia, twelve coal miners tried to shelter themselves from poisonous air. They huddled together deep in the mine, waiting for help. After the explosion, a rescue effort was set in motion. Families gathered to pray and comfort each other.

It's not known when the trapped miners realized they would not make it. We do know that many of them wrote final goodbyes. When word came from rescue workers that only one man had survived, families were in shock. The medical examiner found and distributed the dying men's notes. Each family left to go to their own screaming room.

A brother of one of the deceased miners said the note from his younger brother was both heartbreaking and deeply comforting. His brother, Martin Toler Jr., was the foreman. He was also a man of deep faith who wrote his note on the back of an insurance form. It read: "Tell all I'll see them on the other side."[13]

For Christians, the screaming room is made bearable by the conviction that death is not final. All those who have put their faith in Christ will one day be reunited. And while Martin Toler's note only mentions an "other side," the Scriptures vividly describe it. John writes of a glorious reunion in heaven where God himself will "wipe every tear from their eyes" and there will "be no more death or mourning or crying or pain, for the old order of things has passed away" (Rev 21:4). For the believer, the problem of evil is not a permanent one. One day we will leave the screaming room and be united with a good and loving God.

FURTHER READING

Guinness, Os. *Unspeakable: Facing up to Evil in an Age of Genocide and Terror.* San Francisco: HarperCollins, 2005.

Lewis, C. S. *A Grief Observed.* New York: Bantam, 1976.

Stackhouse, John, Jr. *Can God Be Trusted? Faith and the Challenge of Evil.* New York: Oxford University Press, 1998.

Taylor, Rick. *When Life Is Changed Forever by the Death of Someone Near.* Eugene, Ore.: Harvest House, 1992.

4

Jesus, Buddha or Muhammad?

Seeking a Guide in the Maze of Religions

Consider these facts:

- One out of every five people in the world is Muslim.[1]

- In 1990 there were thirty mosques in the United States. Today there are more than three thousand. On average one new mosque opens each week in the United States.[2]

- From 1990 to 2001, Buddhism grew in the United States by 170 percent and is now the fourth most practiced religion in America.[3] If you Google "Buddhism," you get more than 37 million sites.

- A total of 67 percent of the world's population does not identify itself as Christian.[4]

As Christians we find such information unsettling. How can we claim to have the "truth" when more than four billion people do not

subscribe to the teachings of Christ? To believe that most of the world
is in error feels arrogant and elitist. What right do we have to judge
the faith of others?

How do you respond when a coworker or neighbor asks, "Why
do Christians think they have a corner on the truth?" In a reli-
giously diverse world Christians need to sensitively and confidently
present our conviction that Christ is uniquely qualified to guide us
through today's maze of religions. In the following chapter we'll explore how people view religion today and how we can sensitively
challenge the beliefs of a person who adheres to a faith other than
ours.

HOW PEOPLE THINK ABOUT RELIGION

Today people are put off by caustic religious debates. Believing that
your particular faith has a corner on God can lead to heated arguments, religious persecution, alienation and even war. John Stott explains why we have no patience for groups that claim religious superiority: "The very survival of the human race seems to depend on our
learning to live together in harmony and to cooperate for the common
good. Whatever divides us, therefore, including our religions, is understandably regarded with increasing disfavor."[5]

In order to promote harmony most people today subscribe to the
idea that all religions are different yet equally valid paths to God. Does
this view of religion work? Are all religions merely different paths
heading in the same direction? Or is there a better way to think about
differing faiths? And if so, what is it?

When the issue of religion comes up with a friend or coworker,
consider presenting two different ways to view our pursuit of God.
The first illustration focuses on the perceived goal of differing religions—finding God. This illustration is often referred to as the *mountain paths analogy.*

ALL PATHS LEAD TO GOD

God resides on top of a steep mountain. At the base of the mountain are individuals who try to get up to him by taking different paths. Some paths are winding, while others take a more direct route. Eventually all converge at the same location—God.

The mistake travelers sometimes make is to become overly attached to a particular path. With each step up the mountain, they start to believe that their path is the best or only way to the top. Travelers fail to realize that all paths are equally valid ways to get to the summit.

Ask your friend what he or she thinks of this analogy. Does he or she believe it paints an accurate picture of our pursuit of God?

Before criticizing the analogy, point out its merits. The strength of the mountain paths analogy is that it acknowledges the diversity and sincerity of different religious faiths. Each religion has a unique history behind it and sincere followers who are traveling on its path.

The weakness of this analogy is that it ignores two truths. It fails to take seriously the claims made by various religious figures and glosses over the contradictions among world religions. Let's explore each of these weaknesses.

Weakness 1: The mountain paths analogy alters the claims of key religious figures. How would Muhammad respond to the mountain paths analogy? Did he view Islam as merely one path leading to God? Hardly.

Muhammad taught his followers that the angel Gabriel appeared to him through a series of visions and gave him Allah's final and definitive communication to humans. The central belief of Islam is that salvation is found only in surrender to Allah. In order to be a true follower of Allah, a Muslim must publicly recite, "There is no God but Allah, and Muhammad is the prophet of Allah." To refuse to do so is to ensure separation from Allah.

Muhammad would scoff at the idea that Islam is merely one path to God.

Jesus is just as adamant in claiming that his view is the true path to God. On one occasion Jesus told his followers that he was "the way and the truth and the life" and that a person could not come to God but through him (Jn 14:6). The mountain paths analogy takes Christ's words and strips them of their forcefulness. Advocates of the mountain paths analogy claim that Jesus meant that he was *one way among many* and *a truth for some*. Jesus would strenuously disagree.

Religious giants such as Jesus and Muhammad would rather you think their views wrong than to water them down to make them fit the analogy we've been considering.

The mountain paths analogy is often a convenient position for people uninterested in and uninformed about religion. It's convenient because it provides justification for people's indifference and ignorance so they don't have to change.

Not all faiths, however, would reject the mountain paths analogy. For example, followers of Hinduism would agree with the basic premise of the mountain paths analogy.

Hindus argue that all truth can be blended together so that even opposing beliefs can coexist.[6] This belief, called syncretism, serves as the central, yet unspoken, claim of the mountain paths analogy: "All religions are true, especially Hinduism." The only way for the mountain paths analogy to work is to radically alter the beliefs of Muhammad and Jesus so that they will fit under a Hindu view of religion. A popular Hindu teacher writes that if a Christian were to approach him for guidance, he would not ask the person to abandon a belief in Christ. He *would* ask the Christian to expand his or her view of Christ to one that mirrors the inclusive Supreme Reality at the heart of Hinduism. For all its claims toward neutrality, the mountain paths analogy decidedly favors an Eastern take on God.

Weakness 2: The mountain paths analogy fails to deal with glaring contradictions between religions. Central to the mountain paths analogy is the belief that all religions are the same in their core beliefs, thus making them equally valid paths to God. Is this true? When we compare differing religions, do we find agreements or disagreements?

Any serious study of the core truths of differing religions will quickly reveal that they disagree on key issues: What is the purpose of life? Why is there so much suffering? What separates us from God? What is God like?

To highlight the contradictions between religions, we suggest you and your friend consider one simple question: Who waits for you at the top of the mountain?

Buddhists: No one waits at the top. Buddhists do not acknowledge any deity or god. When world religious leaders came together to create an ethics document to guide our morally confused world, the document ironically did not mention God. The term was left out in order to honor the beliefs of Buddhist contributors.[7]

DIGGING DEEPER

The law of noncontradiction is one of the most fundamental rules of logic. Aristotle, the philosopher most closely associated with the law of noncontradiction, reminds us that when thinking about an issue we must avoid contradicting ourselves. We should not answer a question by saying both yes and no. Consider the question, is your mother still alive? Your answer cannot be both yes and no. She is either alive or not.

This rule of logic is useful when considering the claims of various religions. If one religion claims God does not exist (Buddhism) and another claims he does (Islam), then these two contradictory claims cannot be true at the same time in the same way. For logic, mathematics and meaningful religious communication to work, the law of noncontradiction must be assumed. Even those who deny the universal application of the law of noncontradiction must use it in their denial. If someone says, "The law of noncontradiction is a Western construction," that person is assuming that his or her assertion is contradictory to the statement "The law of non-contradiction is not a Western construction."

Hindus: Thousands of gods and goddesses wait for you at the top.[8] Central to Hindu spirituality is the worship of a multitude of gods and goddesses, who are represented in sacred pictures, idols, images and figurines.

Muslims: Only one God waits at the top. To claim that more than one God, let alone thousands, sits at the top violates the greatest conviction of a Muslim—that Allah is one (Sura 112:1-4). Muslims do not even call Allah "Father," because it implies he has a partner or son.

Jews: Only one God waits at the top. YHWH—the God of Moses, Abraham and the children of Israel—resides alone at the summit.

Christians: At the top of the mountain stands one God. Within the unity of that one God there are three coequal and coeternal persons: God the Father, God the Son and God the Holy Spirit.

Ask your friend what he or she makes of these differences. Is there one God, no God or thousands of gods at the top of the mountain? Common sense tells us that these three answers cannot all be equally true. Even where there appears to be agreement, there is disagreement. While Islam, Judaism and Christianity argue that only one God sits at the top, Muslims and Jews strongly disagree with the Christian concept of the Trinity.[9] If these different views of God cannot be reconciled, then does the mountain paths analogy work?

A DIFFERENT WAY TO LOOK AT RELIGION

Once your concerns about the mountain paths analogy have been discussed, offer to your friend a different illustration, one that honors the complex differences we've just considered. Rather than viewing religions as paths leading up a mountain, why not view religions as a maze with paths heading in different directions?[10]

A MULTIRELIGION MAZE

The most famous maze in the world is located in the gardens of Hampton Court near London. The maze, consisting of eight-foot hedges, was planted in 1702. It covers a third of an acre and its winding paths are more than a half mile long. When entering the maze, you immediately face a choice—which path should you take? The goal is to reach the center of the maze, but which path will take you there? Some routes quickly lead to a dead end; others take you deep into the maze before failing. Some paths run parallel to each other for long periods of time, only to have one hit a wall while the other continues. The challenge is to find the *one* path that leads you to the final destination—the center.

Suggest to your friend that you believe this analogy works better than the mountain paths illustration for several reasons.

First, the maze illustration places a value on exploration and self-discovery. The only way to assess the effectiveness of a route is to consider where it takes you. Does the route lead you to a dead end or take you to the center? The serious seeker of God needs to carefully assess the different routes endorsed by competing religions. What deficiencies found in a route will cause the seeker to abandon this route and look for another?

Second, viewing religions as a maze with multiple routes heading in different directions acknowledges the wildly contradictory views of religions we've just considered. In a maze, participants are confronted with choices that will send them in completely different directions. Heading into the maze, the participant accepts the challenge of finding the one path that will lead him or her to the center.

Third, as in any maze, some routes will at times head in the same direction or run parallel to each other. The Muslim, Jewish and Christian routes run parallel to each other in their belief that God is one (monotheism). Hinduism and Buddhism run parallel to each other in their belief in the laws of karma and reincarnation. The maze illustration lets travelers acknowledge similarities as paths head in the same direction, even though only one will ultimately arrive at the center.

BUILDING BRIDGES

After presenting the maze illustration, you may be tempted to rush to point out to your friend the dead ends you believe exist in his or her religion. This could be a mistake. What you view as a dead end could be a sacred belief to your friend.

A friend of ours once recounted a story of his visit to the Dome of the Rock in Jerusalem. He became separated from his tour group and wandered off by himself. Rounding a corner, he was suddenly confronted by a very angry guard wielding a submachine gun. He found it impossible to communicate with the guard; all he could do was stand very still with his hands in the air. In his ignorance he had done much more than trespass—he had violated a sacred place. We risk invoking an equally angry response if we rashly confront and possibly violate a person's most cherished beliefs.

Our job as Christian communicators is to unearth the cherished beliefs of a neighbor or friend. Once we have discovered a belief, we need to ask crucial questions: What is the best way to acknowledge the sacred and the feelings associated with it? How can we sensitively discuss the beliefs of others? If we rush to critique the beliefs of others, we risk making them defensive. And as Proverbs teaches, an offended person is harder to win than a fortified city (Prov 18:19).

We mentioned earlier that the strength of the maze illustration is that it's possible for travelers to acknowledge when routes in the maze head in the same direction. This recognition is fostered when we acknowledge how the teachings of other faiths mirror Christian values. Being a Christian does not keep us from commending acts of compassion or activism by followers of other religions. There is much we can learn from non-Christians who have great practical wisdom or an admirable lifestyle. The most affirming thing we can do with those of differing faiths is to acknowledge individuals central to their faith. The following illustrations show how followers of different faiths can share similar values and ask the same questions as Christians.

THE COMPASSION OF MAHATMA GANDHI

In Gandhi's lifetime the caste system of India was in full force. At the bottom of the system were poor farmers, laborers, meat handlers and scavengers. These people were segregated from the general population and lived with the label Untouchables. They were forbidden to enter temples, sit at public tables or even allow their shadow to touch others.

Risking political and personal alienation, Gandhi took up the cause of the Untouchables. His first act was to change their name from Untouchables to Harijans (Children of God). He not only associated with them but even caused a public outcry by inviting an Untouchable to live with him. He looked for every opportunity to show his solidarity with the poor and alienated. At the height of popularity, Gandhi was asked by reporters why he chose to travel third class with India's outcasts when he could travel first class with British dignitaries. He responded that he traveled third class because there was no fourth class. Such compassion made an impression on Christian author Philip Yancey. He writes, "Gandhi devoted his life to recognize the inherent dignity in every human being. He strove to devote the same care in making a mudpack for a leprosy victim as in conducting an interview with the Viceroy of India."[11]

Compassion toward those in need is also shared by Muslims. Muhammad, himself once poor and an orphan, makes giving to those in need one of the five pillars of Islam. Muslims are required to give a portion of their income to help orphans, widows and the sick within the Muslim community. Christians resonate with a concern for the needy and are reminded that "pure and faultless" religion in God's sight is to "look after orphans and widows in their distress" (Jas 1:27).[12]

BUDDHA'S INSIGHTFUL QUESTIONS

Though we know him by his title, Buddha (meaning "awakened one"), his name is Gautama Siddhartha. Legend states that he was a child prince who was sequestered by his father in a luxurious palace. This inquisitive youth bribed his handler to allow him to travel outside the palace. Outside the confines of luxury, he saw what Buddhists refer to as the Four Distressing Sights: a sick man, an old man, a dying man and a wise man who forsook everything to pursue wisdom. These sights led Buddha to some of life's most disturbing *why* questions: "Why do we suffer?" "Can suffering be avoided?" "What is wisdom?" "How should one live?"

Siddhartha left the palace and spent his life seeking answers. Buddhists know his conclusions as the Four Noble Truths: Life is suffering; suffering is caused by selfish desire; suffering ceases as desire ceases; suffering ceases when our egos are transformed.

Buddhists and non-Buddhists alike have recognized Buddha's profound insights and attempts to wrestle with suffering. Catholic philosopher Peter Kreeft argues that most people today view Buddha as the second most profound thinker in human history, trailing only Jesus. Kreeft writes, "Buddha's entire philosophy centers around his answer to the problem of suffering. Whether that philosophy is true or false, here is a man who descended deep, deep into the mystery of suffering. How can we not hear him out?"[13]

Yet few Christians study Buddha's wrestling with suffering, because we ultimately reject many of his answers.[14] Such a reaction ignores an insight offered by C. S. Lewis: "The man who agrees with us that some question, little regarded by others, is of great importance can be our friend. He need not agree with us about some answer."[15] Although we may reject Buddha's answers, we can appreciate his questions. The questions Buddha wrestles with are the very ones we all wrestle with in times of deep struggle: Why is there suffering? How can I cope with so much pain? What can I do to elevate personal suffering in the future?

Why is it important to acknowledge the accomplishments and thoughts of other religious leaders? First, if we ignore the ideas and lives of key religious leaders, then we invite a frustrated response from others. Nobel Prize winner Desmond Tutu voiced this frustration: "Gandhi was not a Christian, but if you say Gandhi was not a good man, you are not speaking my language." Second, in most conversations people tend to treat you the way you treat them. If we want persons of a different faith to listen to *our* story, then we must listen to theirs. If we want others to attend to *our* convictions, then we must first attend to theirs. If we desire for others to cul-

DIGGING DEEPER

Repeatedly, Scripture acknowledges the wisdom of peoples outside Israel—the Edomites (Jer 49:7), the Phoenicians (Zech 9:2) and many others. Job 28:1-11 acknowledges remarkable achievements produced by human wisdom. Scripture compares the wisdom of Solomon to that of the "men of the East" and Egypt in order to show that it surpassed that of peoples with long-standing, well-deserved reputations for wisdom (1 Kings 4:29-34). Paul approvingly quotes pagan philosophers (Acts 17:28).

For John Wesley, the study of extrabiblical information and the writings of unbelievers was of critical value for growth and maturity. "To imagine none can teach you but those who are themselves saved from sin, is a very great and dangerous mistake."[16]

tivate common ground with our faith, we must do so first. In doing so we will create a communication climate that will allow us to gently probe truths central to their faith.

DETERMINING WHERE A PATH LEADS

In previous conversations you've discussed with your friend the merits of the maze illustration and your appreciation of individuals such as Gandhi or Buddha. In this conversation you may want to discuss a key part of the maze illustration—the fact that not all routes make it to the center of the maze. Some routes, while going deep into the maze, hit a dead end. No doubt this could be an awkward point in the conversation. Make sure to preface your comments by saying that it's obviously one's opinion whether a trail hits a dead end or not. In the following we briefly explore Buddhism and Islam to determine whether there is a dead end.

Starting a Conversation: Concerns with Buddhism. While Buddha's probing of suffering is profound, we feel Buddhism hits a dead end when it comes to the law of karma. Simply put, the law of karma entails the belief that what a person reaps in this life, good or bad, is the result of actions committed in his or her previous life. The Dalai Lama, Buddhism's most recognizable spokesperson, explains, "Frankly speaking, my own happiness is mainly due to my own good karma. It is a fundamental Buddhist belief that my own suffering is due to my mistakes."[17]

If the law of karma is true, then all of us would feel the burden of trying to make amends for all our bad actions. It's a weight felt deeply by TV's most unlikely hero.

MY NAME IS EARL—KARMA 101

The hit series *My Name Is Earl* focuses on the life of a social misfit named Earl. Earl's life has been one bad choice after another. After finding out he's won a small lottery, he's immediately hit by a car and finds himself in the hospital. While lying in a hospital bed, he has a "karmic epiphany" and decides to make a "karma list" of all the bad things (three hundred of them) he's done in life. His hope is that if he does good things to the people he's mistreated, he'll rack up good karma. A sampling of his list includes:

1: Stole $10 from a guy in Camden Market.

23: *Never* giving Mom a "Mother's Day" card.

50: Failing to pay taxes.

64: Picked on Kenny Jones in elementary school.

74: Gave ex-wife thoughtless Christmas gifts.

147: Shot Gwen Waters with BB gun.

While Earl's list and intentions make for good TV, Earl forgets a significant truth about karma—it's impossible to negate the impact of evil actions by doing good actions.[18] Regardless of how many good acts Earl does, he will still experience, in this life or the next, the unavoidable consequences of his bad actions. As soon as a person engages in a bad act, he or she can only brace himself or herself for the negative *re*action. Such a view produces in many adherents to Buddhism a fatalistic view of life. All of us, like Earl, could compile a list of bad actions. If we took the Buddhist position, life could be a constant process of trying to limit our misdeeds and resigning ourselves to the inevitable negative consequences when we do fail.

How can we get out of the endless cycle of cause and effect brought on by bad karma?

Bono, social activist and lead singer of U2, explains that what drew him to Christ was the idea that the law of karma could be counteracted by grace.

I'd be in big trouble if karma was going to finally be my judge. I'm holding out for grace. I'm holding out that Jesus took my sins onto the cross, because I know who I am, and I hope I don't

have to depend on my own religiosity. . . . The point of the death
of Christ is that Christ took on the sins of the world, so that
what we put out did not come back to us, that our sinful nature
does not reap the obvious death.[19]

One other concern about Buddhism deserves mention. While
many Buddhists are compassionate social activists, the law of karma
seems to put them in a difficult intellectual corner. After interviewing
the Dalai Lama, Jim Beverly was both impressed and troubled by what
he had learned. Beverly notes:

> The Dalai Lama writes in one of his books that a person killed
> by a lightning bolt has earned that fate by some misdeed in a pre-
> vious life. That example, though grim, does not address the
> deeper implications of the Buddhist view. Consider the nuns
> raped by Communist soldiers during the purge of Tibet. What
> was their karmic debt?[20]

While Buddhists would passionately denounce rape, what role
does bad karma play in the victimization of an individual over another? What role does karma play in the plight of the poor? The oppressed? In a conversation with a Buddhist friend, gently pursue these
issues. The goal is to have a dialogue that both respects and challenges
the beliefs of others.

No one can force another to concede that a worldview has come to
an end in the maze of faith. You can only offer reasons why you have
committed to one route over another.

Starting a Conversation: Concerns with Islam. The duty of a Muslim is to obey and serve Allah. Salvation is secured through a lifetime
of effort. On the day of God's judgment a person's good deeds will be
weighed against his or her bad deeds. "Those whose balance [of good
deeds] is heavy, they will attain salvation, but those whose balance is

light, will be those who have lost their souls; in Hell will they abide"
(Sura 23:102-103). How many good deeds does a person need to ac-
cumulate to feel good about his or her chances of going to heaven?
What if a person has a lapse of faith in his or her spiritual journey?
Can a Muslim ever feel confident that heaven awaits him or her?

NO GUARANTEE

Author Lorraine Orris shares the story of a devout Muslim wrestling with a lack of certainty concerning salvation.

> I was born in Saudi Arabia as a member of a Muslim family.
> We were a very happy family, and I loved my relationship
> with them. I was always very serious to do all that God or-
> dered me to do—fasting on Ramadan, praying five times a
> day or more, and so on. I, at that time, very much desired
> to meet God at the last day, even when I had no guarantee.
>
> After some time my life became very hard. Slowly I
> drifted far away from God. My life became busy. I had a
> very good job and earned a lot of money. Still, I was not
> happy because I was afraid for the day that I would die.
> Sometimes a question came to my mind—will I be with
> God in heaven or not? And it was frightening to think
> about this, even for seconds, that I would not be there.[21]

This experience is common for many Muslims. After paraphrasing
this testimony, point out to your friend that a Muslim has no guarantee of heaven or Allah's favor. Even when he is doing well in his faith,
he can't be certain he will go to heaven.

Most of us can relate to this man's lapse of faith. Few people go
through their religious journey without some struggles when our faith
wanes and we drift from God. In a Muslim worldview such times can
be costly when judgment day arrives.

Christian philosopher David Clark calls this a *contractual view* of religion. "People enter a fee-for-service arrangement with God. The human gives money, does religious rituals and believes religious ideas. In return, she expects protection, help, good fortune, a sense of meaning of life and rescue from punishment in the next life."[22] The problem with a contractual view of religion is, what if I don't hold up my part of the contract? What assurance can I have that I am fulfilling my end of the deal? In the previous testimony such questions produced fear: "Will I be with God in heaven or not?"

Clark compares this view with a *covenant view* of religion found in Christianity. "In a covenantal relationship, I live a good life because I'm responding faithfully to the gift of love. Like a groom who remains faithful to his bride, I follow God's will not to gain love but because he first loved me."[23]

Central to a Christian view of God is the idea of *grace,* powerfully described by the apostle Paul: "It is by grace you have been saved, through faith—and this not from yourselves, it is the gift of God—not by works, so that no one can boast" (Eph 2:8-9). Christians are well aware that we cannot hold up our end of a spiritual contract with God. While religious devotion is key, our salvation does not rest on it. In Christ, God loves us in the valleys as well as the heights in our pursuit of him.

BLAZING A NEW TRAIL

So far in this chapter we've been discussing well-worn paths in the maze of faith such as Islam, Buddhism and Christianity. Many individuals take comfort in following paths that millions of people have walked before them. Yet others want to chart their own spiritual course. These are friends who wouldn't identify themselves as Buddhist, Christian or Muslim. The last thing they want is to be restricted to one path. They want to pursue God on their own terms.

In a *Newsweek* poll discussing spirituality in America, respondents said they felt the strongest connection with God when they were praying alone (40 percent), while 21 percent said they felt the strongest connection to God in a house of worship. Only 27 percent described their religious practices as "very traditional." When asked if someone of a different faith can attain salvation or get to heaven, 79 percent of respondents said yes.[24]

The more Americans embrace individualism and relativism, the more we feel the freedom to mix and match different faiths. In his book *The Divine Deli,* John Berthrong writes that "traditional boundaries" between religions are dissolving and people feel the freedom to have "multiple citizenships" in a number of faiths.[25]

Vietnamese columnist Anh Do describes her upbringing as a multiple citizen of diverse religious faiths.

> My father filled our home with books and music, making sure we had information on the Koran, Hinduism, Confucianism, Quakers and Jehovah's Witness. My mother took us to temple, cooked kosher and navigated us through First Communion all the while garbing us in the right clothes to match secular holidays. Both parents showed us that practicing is believing, yet that there's always more than one belief.[26]

To an individual like Ms. Do, religions are like a wonderfully exotic buffet where we are free to pick and choose as we see fit.

How should we respond? Consider presenting an illustration that addresses the dangers of piecing together your own religious worldview.

BUFFET RELIGION

We as Americans have become increasingly aware of our expanding waistlines. While many culprits have been suspected, one particular activity has caught the attention of researchers—buffet dining.

You know how it works. For one price you can have as much as you want of whatever you fancy. The choices are endless and require quick decisions. Your plate fills up as you work the line. You pay for an overflowing plate and dig in. If someone would analyze your plate, he or she would have a good idea of your likes and dislikes. Your plate is filled with pastas, desserts, breads and deep-fried anything, with green leafy things glaringly absent. Obesity expert Robert Jeffery states that all-you-can-eat buffets play into our human propensity to eat too much and favor what we want over what we need.[27]

The same is true in mixing and matching religions. When borrowing from a particular religion, we take the aspects of it we like and pass over the parts that are too demanding or make us uncomfortable. Many find the practice of meditation in Buddhism appealing, but they bypass the Buddha's commitment to a life of simplicity and strong admonishment to eliminate desire. People are attracted to Christianity's emphasis on God's love but want nothing to do with his command to pursue lives of sacrifice and purity. When we form our own religious worldview, we end up with nothing but a projection of our own likes and dislikes, a personalized religion that never requires us to abandon much of what we already believe or like. Conveniently, God ends up looking exactly like the person who went looking for him. We create God in our own image, not the other way around.

Are we qualified to create our own religious worldview? Few of us would feel confident in performing surgery on ourselves or building our own computer from scratch; what makes us think we are qualified to create our own religious path?

COMMON RELIGIOUS DESIRE

For all our diversity, Americans are united in the value we place on spirituality. Only 8 percent of respondents from the *Newsweek* poll said they were not religious or spiritual. We can be assured that matters of faith, spirituality and God are present concerns of our coworkers, family and friends. Most of us, at some level, have entered the maze of faith. Are we on our own or is there someone who knows the way? What qualifications would such a guide need? Can these credentials be checked out? These are the questions we'll consider in the next chapter.

5

Jesus, Buddha or Muhammad? (Part 2)

Over three hundred thousand people a year go into the Hampton Court maze to gladly get turned around and disoriented. When the maze first opened to the public in the 1700s, some visitors would get hopelessly lost. Guides had to follow their cries to find them in order to lead them out. That problem doesn't exist today. An attendant now stands on a platform high above the maze. From his or her vantage point, the attendant can shout down to lost visitors and serve as their guide.

Christians believe that God, like the attendant above the maze, knows which paths lead to a dead end and which one leads to him. God isn't content to shout down from a platform to guide and direct us. He came down in the person of Christ to be our guide. It is a foundational Christian belief that in Christ "all the fullness of the Deity lives in bodily form" (Col 2:9). From his divine vantage point, Jesus can reveal to us which path God created to lead us through the maze.

In the previous chapter we discussed the importance of acknowledging the insights of religious figures who have blazed a trail in the maze. Taking time to focus on the contributions of other religious leaders gives you credibility to speak about the life of Christ and what establishes him to be the authoritative guide.

LIFE OF JESUS

What convinced the early followers of Christ that he was God? How did they come by a conviction so firm that the early followers of Christ endured persecution, hardship and even death to follow him? What stood out to them were not only the claims he made about himself but also the miracles that accompanied those claims. In the Gospels we see dramatic displays of Christ's qualifications to lead people to God in the maze of faith. Consider four powerful illustrations.

Qualification 1: Claim to divinity. According to Jesus, his greatest qualification for being able to lead people to God is that he and God are one. Keep in mind that Jesus said this in the context of monotheism, not pantheism. He wasn't saying that he, like all of us, is God in some general sense. No, he was saying that he is the one and only Creator God, distinct from all creation. It was as shocking a claim then as it is now.

I AM

In one of his many debates with religious leaders, Jesus makes a statement that puts his life in danger. This one statement by Jesus sends his opponents into a rage as they pick up rocks to kill him. What does he say? Jesus utters the divine name of God given to Moses.

In the book of Exodus, Moses is having a crisis of confidence. He wants to know the name of God so he'll have credibility as God's chosen leader. God responds, "This is what you are to say to the Israelites: 'I AM has sent me to you' " (Ex 3:14). The name I AM communicated that God is the eternal, timeless Creator of everything. This name became so sacred that Jews would seldom utter it.

Jesus not only speaks God's divine name but also uses it to refer to himself! He states that although Abraham was a great man, he existed before him. "Before Abraham was born, I am!" (John 8:58). The Jews were not confused by his statement. For brazenly applying the name of God to himself, Jesus could, under the law, be put to death (Lev 24:16). When the crowd tries to take him, Jesus eludes them. On another occasion Jesus proclaims to a crowd outside Jerusalem, "I and the Father are one" (Jn 10:30). The Jews again pick up stones and charge him with blasphemy: "You, a mere man, claim to be God" (Jn 10:33).

After sharing this illustration, point out that this claim is unique to Jesus. Muhammad readily admitted that he was only a prophet of Allah, while Buddha acknowledged that he was merely a man seeking enlightenment. If Jesus is who he claims to be, then each path in the maze is trying to *get to him*. He himself is ultimately the main point of all his teaching. He knows exactly at what point a path hits a dead end and which one is successful.

Qualification 2: Jesus' ability to forgive sins. If Jesus is who he claims to be, then he has the power and authority to forgive sin. From adulterers to prostitutes to shifty tax gatherers to crucified felons, Jesus regularly bestowed forgiveness on those most desperate to receive it.

POWER TO FORGIVE

While Jesus is speaking to a group in a house, he hears a noise above him. He looks up to see a man being lowered on a mat through a hole in the roof. The man is paralyzed and his friends have taken desperate measures to bring him to Jesus' attention. It works. Jesus responds to the man before him: "Friend, your sins are forgiven" (Lk 5:20).

A gasp goes up from Jesus' critics. Claming to forgive sins is blasphemy. Jesus knows what they are thinking and decides to give them an object lesson. He asks if they think it's easier to forgive sins or ask a paralyzed man to walk. No one dares answer. Jesus tells the man to pick up his mat and go home. To the astonishment of all, the man does. The implication is clear: the same power used to heal this man also was used to forgive sins.

Jesus' adversaries are outraged because Jesus is claiming to do what only God can do—forgive the sins of others. In life we are limited to forgiving actions committed against *us*. If I forgive someone who has hurt you, how would you react? You would be angry. What gives *you* the right to forgive a person who has sinned against *me*? Jesus understands that all sin, no matter who is involved, is ultimately a sin against God. Since Jesus is God, he has the divine prerogative to forgive anyone. Point out to your friend that Jesus' claim to forgive sins is accompanied by a miracle that verifies his claim.

Jesus' claim to forgive again sets him apart. Muhammad would shun the idea that he could forgive the sins of others. Buddha was powerless to negate the effects of bad karma for him or others. Yet Jesus regularly says to others, "I forgive you."

Qualification 3: Ability to perform miracles and delegate this power to his followers to perform miracles in his name. In quick succession the Gospel of Mark shows Jesus' ability to work miracles. He calms a violent storm at sea (Mk 4:39), heals a demon-possessed man (Mk 5:13) and cures a woman of a previously incurable blood disease (Mk 5:34). Mark then describes a miracle that shocks even his closest followers.

POWER OVER DEATH

A frantic father falls at the feet of Jesus. His twelve-year-old daughter is dying. He begs Jesus to come and lay his hands on her to heal her. As he is pleading for his daughter's life, word comes that she has died and he needs to return home. Jesus accompanies the father home and makes an astonishing statement when they arrive: "The child is not dead but asleep" (Mk 5:39). Those mourning the death of this little girl respond angrily to Jesus' seemingly insensitive comment. But Jesus escorts the parents to the girl's side. Jesus takes her hand and says, "Little girl, I say to you, get up!" (Mk 5:41). And she does! With one simple command, Jesus brings this girl back to life. Mark tells us that her parents were completely astonished. How could they not be?

It's interesting to note that the adversaries of Christ didn't dispute that he performed miracles. Rather, they argued that he did so through magic or satanic power. In the next chapter we'll consider a miracle that serves as the verification of all his claims—Christ's own resurrection.

Miraculous healings have also continued to be performed in Jesus' name throughout the history of Jesus' church. The *Washington Times* recently featured a story on the explosion of Christianity in China.[1] The author notes that the underground church alone contains as least 100 million believers, compared to 70 million members of the Communist Party. Why is Christianity growing? "One of the driving forces of Christianity's growth in China has been its association with healing powers, particularly in rural areas where basic health services are lacking." The article cites the case of a young woman who had contracted a virus doctors had never seen before. She was on a ventilator and everyone had lost hope for her recovery. But following prayer, she was healed and fully recovered. As a result, "now her family follows Christ, too."

Qualification 4: Ability to guarantee salvation. Muslims live their entire lives with uncertainty about their eternal destination. How will they fare under Allah's judgment? Hindus resign themselves to an endless cycle of rebirth in which their future lives are determined by good and bad karma.

Perhaps the most important qualification of Christ we can present to a person is his authority to grant salvation *now.*

HEAVEN ASSURED!

Crucifixion is as painful as it is efficient. Luke tells us that Jesus hung with two other men, both criminals (Lk 23:32). When the Romans instituted the punishment of crucifixion, it had clear restrictions. Only slaves or foreigners convicted of murder, rebellion and armed robbery were subjected to such a barbaric death. Only in extreme cases of treason would a Roman citizen be a possible candidate for crucifixion.

The men Christ died with were bad men. However, as the drama plays out, one of the criminals starts to soften. He acknowledges that he deserves his punishment. He understands that Christ is not only innocent but in fact is who he claims to be—God. He turns to Jesus and says, "Remember me when you come into your kingdom" (Lk 23:42).

Jesus responds to his plea for salvation and assures him, "Today you will be with me in paradise" (Lk 23:43).

What's important to highlight in this illustration is how hopeless the situation would be for this criminal in other religious systems. According to Islam, he would have little hope of salvation. As a criminal, one worthy of crucifixion, his bad deeds would surely outweigh his good deeds when judged by Allah. For Muslims there is no grace to appeal to on the day of judgment. According to Buddhism, the criminal's bad karma would ensure another negative rebirth. Yet in Luke's account this man is forgiven. He doesn't have to do anything but receive God's forgiveness offered through Christ. Upon his death he enters heaven with his Christ.

The uniqueness of Christ described in these four illustrations is why other religions hold Jesus in such high regard. Hindus and Buddhists regard him as an enlightened teacher, while Muslims acknowledge him as one of Islam's greatest prophets.[2]

After presenting these descriptions of Jesus, ask your friend what he or she makes of him. Based on what your friend has just heard, is Jesus qualified to be our guide out of the maze of faith? At this point in the conversation it's crucial to make sure your friend is consistent in answering the question. The next section presents limited options in how we can respond to the claims and credentials of Jesus.

WHAT TO DO WITH JESUS?

What are we to make of the claims of Christ? Is he God? Does he have the authority to forgive? Is he a miracle worker? The claims of Christ put us in an awkward position.

DIGGING DEEPER

Christians are often confronted with the following: "You think Jesus is unique, rather than Buddha or Muhammad, because you were raised in a Christian country and your parents taught you to prefer Christianity to Buddhism or Islam." This claim reflects what is known as the *genetic fallacy*. This fallacy occurs when someone confuses the origin of an idea with the reasons for believing the idea and faults the idea because of where it came from ("my parents taught it to me") and not because of the adequacy of the grounds for maintaining the belief (for example, the reliability of the Bible, historical proof for the resurrection, a personal experience of God and so on). We need to keep separate a psychological or originating *why* from a rational *why*. Just because your parents taught you that two plus two equals four, and not five, doesn't mean that it's not true!

LIAR, LUNATIC OR TIME TRAVELER?

Macedonia is an archaeologist's dream. It's the home of mythic gods such as Zeus and conquering heroes such as Alexander the Great. Pasko Kuzman is one of Macedonia's most respected and quirky archaeologists. His academic credentials are impeccable and his knack for finding archaeological treasures is uncanny. He has also raised quite a stir. The controversy centers upon three watches he wears on his left wrist. Pasko claims they are time machines that allow him to travel to the past or future. He knows so much about the Bronze Age because he's *been there*.

What are we to make of this self-professed time traveler? First, we can conclude that he is lying. His claims are harmless fibs designed to draw attention to an often overlooked profession. Second, we can believe he's mentally unstable. Pasko really believes that he can manipulate time and that he has firsthand knowledge of the Neolithic Age. But if we conclude he's slightly unstable, how much does that weaken our confidence in him as an expert? Or we can conclude that he is what he claims to be—the first-ever time traveler. He alone can predict the future and settle all our nagging historical questions. If his claim is true, he would be the most sought-after person in the world by historians and stockbrokers alike.

The assertions made by Jesus make Pasko's claims look like child's play.

Christ didn't claim to be able to traverse time; he claimed to have existed *before* time. While we marvel at the accomplishments of Alexander the Great, Christ claimed to be the Creator of Alexander and the one who has authority to judge his soul. Christ didn't claim to know about gods like Zeus; he stated unequivocally that he *is* the one true God. In the case of Pasko, we can overlook his claim of time travel as the overactive imagination of a gifted archeologist. It's not so easy to do so with Christ's claims. Was he lying when he said he could forgive sins or assure a person of salvation? Such a lie would be morally reprehensible. Was he a lunatic? Did he really believe that he was God and that his teachings were divine? Or is he who he claims to be—God?

The one thing we must avoid is believing that Jesus was a liar or a lunatic and *still* a good moral teacher.[3] You can't have it both ways. C. S. Lewis forcefully writes:

> You must make a choice. This was and is the Son of God: or else a madman: or something worse. You can shut him up for a fool: you can spit at him and kill him as a demon: or you can fall at his feet and call him Lord and God. But don't come to him with any of that patronizing nonsense about his being a great human teacher. He hasn't left that open to you. He didn't intend to.[4]

OBJECTIONS

While you are discussing the maze illustration and the claims of Christ, a friend or coworker may raise two possible objections. The first objection focuses on the dissension the maze illustration could foster among religions. The second probes disturbing implications of Christ's being the only way to God.

Objection 1: The evils of evangelism. In his provocative book *Why Christianity Must Change or Die,* liberal theologian John Shelby Spong argues that all attempts to convert people of different faiths are expressions of arrogance and hostility toward those who are different.[5] Today the word *evangelism* is synonymous with fanaticism, arrogance and intolerance. Your friend may argue that the maze illustration will produce the hostility described by Spong as people of different faiths engage in heated arguments, trying to convince each other that their paths are dead ends.

Agree with your friend that it would undesirable to engage in a heated argument about religion. The goal of the maze illustration is to foster productive dialogue—a give-and-take conversation in which differing perspectives are respected, critiqued and sometimes challenged in a spirit of civility. America's history is filled with key, sometimes intense, dialogues about crucial ideas—liberty, race, sexuality, God and so forth. Consider the following illustration that places value on persuasive dialogue.

DECLARATION OF SENTIMENTS

In the early 1800s women were frustrated with their inability to invoke social change in America. Women couldn't vote and had almost no public voice. A key step in achieving basic rights occurred in 1848 in New York City. The Seneca Falls Convention was organized by women's rights activists including Lucretia Coffin Mott, Mary Anne McClintock and Elizabeth Cady Stanton. The key moment at the conference occurred when Stanton delivered a speech called the "Declaration of Sentiments" (modeled after the Declaration of Independence). In part it read, "We hold these truths to be self-evident: that all men and women are created equal; that they are endowed by their Creator with certain inalienable rights, that among these are life, liberty, and the pursuit of happiness."[6]

The speech added fuel to a public dialogue that would ensue for the next seventy-two years and culminate on August 26, 1920, when a constitutional amendment was passed granting women the right to vote. Yet what would Spong say about these women's attempt to persuade others? Would he say that their persuasive communication is an expression of arrogance and hostility toward those who are different? Spong is right to critique any groups, religious or political, if they exhibit hostile attitudes or uncivil communication. But he's wrong to stereotype all religious dialogue designed to persuade as hostile and arrogant. Respectful, thoughtful and persuasive discussions about God are some of the most worthwhile conversations we can have with one another.

Objection 2: What about those who have not had the opportunity to respond to Christ? For many Christians, this is a disturbing implication of our claim that Christ is the only way to God. What do we do with people in the maze of faith who were unaware that there even was a Christian path available?

As with responding to the problem of evil discussed in chapters two and three, keep in mind that it is appropriate to acknowledge to your friend that this is a challenging and disturbing question. For most of us, this issue is unsettling and will require careful study of the Scriptures.[7]

In handling difficult questions such as this, we find it helpful to begin with what we know and move to what is less clear. From the Scriptures it is clear that the love of God extends to all people regardless of geographical location (Jn 3:16). It is equally clear that God desires all people to be saved and to come to a knowledge of the truth (1 Tim 2:4). There is only one mediator between God and man—Jesus Christ (1 Tim 2:5). God's love for the world is so great that he commands his followers to sacrifice everything in taking the Gospel to the entire world (Mt 28:19-20; Mk 16:15-16; Lk 24:46-48; Acts 1:8).

While the Scriptures are clear that Christ is the necessary means of salvation and that one must confess his name to be saved (Rom 10:9-13), what happens to people living where no known missionary has or will travel? Due to the Scriptures' relative silence on this issue, Christians are left to speculate on what will happen to those who have never heard of Christ.[8] Adherents of any one view cannot be fully assured that they possess *the* answer. Christians, however, can be assured of one thing: God will do what is right in the case of those who are unaware of the Christian path. Unlike the decisions of human judges, God's judgment is always informed, unbiased, compassionate and trustworthy. He is the ideal judge.

WHAT A JUDGE OUGHT TO BE

The American Bar Association (ABA) has more than four hundred thousand members and is the largest voluntary professional association in the world. Its purpose is to provide advice to lawyers when encountering difficult situations. One of a lawyer's greatest nightmares is when a judge acts inappropriately.

The ABA lays out a clear picture of how a judge ought to act.

A judge shall respect and comply with the law and shall act at all times in a manner that promotes public confidence in the integrity and impartiality of the judiciary. A judge shall not at any time engage in conduct that reflects adversely on the judge's honesty, impartiality, temperament, or fitness as a judge.[9]

If a judge acts contrary to this description, then a lawyer has legal grounds to file a complaint. The judge has disqualified himself or herself.

After presenting the ABA's description of a model judge, ask your friend where he or she thinks the ABA got the idea of what a perfect judge should look like. Christians believe that our sense of justice and fairness comes from the fact that we are made in the image of a just and fair God (this idea will be fully developed in chapters eight and nine).

While you may not be able to fully answer your friend's objection, you are confident that God is fit to judge. His honesty, compassion and fairness are the source of the ABA's description of a perfect human judge. All people of the world are objects of his love and he is relent-

DIGGING DEEPER

Righteousness is that attribute by which God's nature is seen to be the eternally perfect standard of what is right.

- *"The great God, mighty and awesome, who shows no partiality . . ." (Deut 10:17).*
- *"A faithful God who does no wrong, upright and just is he" (Deut 32:4).*
- *"The LORD is righteous, he loves justice" (Ps 11:7).*
- *"The LORD our God is righteous in everything he does" (Dan 9:14).*

The judges of Israel were commanded to follow God's example and be just in all their judgments:

- *"Do not accept a bribe, for a bribe blinds those who see" (Ex 23:8).*
- *"Do not show partiality in judging; hear both small and great alike. . . . Judgment belongs to God" (Deut 1:17).*

However God decides to judge those who have never heard of Christ, Christians and non-Christians alike can be assured that he will do what is fair and just.[10]

lessly pursuing them. At the time of judgment all people, even those who have never heard of Christ, will acknowledge that God has done what is right (Gen 18:25). There will be no need to file a grievance against him.

CONCLUSION

Just as the keeper above the Hampton Court Maze navigates lost tourists through the maze, God guides us out of the maze of religions through the person of Christ. Jesus' credentials to serve as our guide are unparalleled.

He is the one and only God-man, who died for our sins and was then raised from the dead to authenticate his person and work. And it is this threefold, historical uniqueness which qualifies him to be the Saviour of the world, the only mediator between God and humankind (1 Timothy 2:5). No one else has these qualifications.[11]

In the next chapter we'll consider one qualification—the resurrection—that is embraced by Christians and questioned by skeptics. It is a qualification that, if true, establishes Jesus as the authoritative guide in the maze of faith.

FURTHER READING

Anderson, Norman, ed. *The World's Religions*. Grand Rapids: Eerdmans, 1991.

McDermott, Gerald R. *Can Evangelicals Learn from World Religions?*
Downers Grove, Ill.: InterVarsity Press, 2000.

Nash, Ronald. *Is Jesus the Only Savior?* Grand Rapids: Zondervan,
1994.

The World Next Door Theme Issue of *Discipleship Journal*, September–October 2002.

The Resurrection

Conspiracy Theory or Fact?

Do you love a good conspiracy theory? If so, you're not alone.

In a 1999 Gallup Poll 6 percent of Americans believed that the first moon landing never happened. Many are convinced that a UFO was discovered in 1947 by the Air Force in Roswell, New Mexico, and is now under lock and key. Some Americans claim that the Holocaust, including photos of death camps, was manufactured by the Allied Forces as propaganda against the Nazis.

As a nation weaned on *The Last Temptation of Christ* and *The Da Vinci Code*, we have also become skeptical of religion. Was Jesus married? Did he ever claim to be God? What is the church trying to hide? To some, the mother of all conspiracy theories is the resurrection of Christ. Skeptics argue that the disciples fabricated the story that after his death Jesus miraculously rose from the dead. It was an elaborate hoax that gave rise to the Christian faith.

How can we respond to such a challenge?

When you are asked to explain your belief in the resurrection, we suggest you offer two lines of proof: your personal experience of Christ and historical evidence.[1] First, describe to your friend what it means to have a personal relationship with Christ. We know Christ has risen from the dead because we experience his presence. Describe to your friend the times you've felt Christ's peace in the midst of difficulty or times you've prayed to Christ and seen dramatic answers. The proof that Christ has risen from the dead is not just relegated to intellectual arguments. Christians experience Christ's peace, love and care on a daily basis.

However, we don't believe in Christ's resurrection just because of personal experience. We also believe in the resurrection because it makes the most sense of historical facts. Challenges to the resurrection, when carefully examined, aren't convincing. Conspiracy theories are fun to consider but crumble when confronted with the evidence. In the next section we'll consider three challenges to the resurrection.

OBJECTION TO THE RESURRECTION: A WELL-PLANNED LIE

Many people dismiss the disciples' claim to have seen the risen Christ as a lie. Such a reaction is understandable since we live in a time when we've been lied to by politicians, clergy, sports figures and presidents. Not only have we become jaded to the truth; we've also become adept at spotting lies. If a lie is weak or poorly constructed, it won't last long in today's skeptical culture. The problem with this objection is that if the disciples lied about the resurrection, then their lie violated everything we know about *effective* lies.

In the following we offer five steps to telling an effective lie. As you present these to your friend, it will become obvious that the disciples botch each step. They are, it turns out, terrible liars.

How to tell an effective lie (step 1): Tell only those lies that benefit you. Seems obvious, doesn't it? The reason we tells lies is to gain some type of advantage or benefit. This is a lesson Frank Abagnale learned at a young age and perfected in adulthood.

CATCH ME IF YOU CAN

Frank Abagnale (played by Leonardo DiCaprio) was a master con artist who served as the inspiration for the movie *Catch Me If You Can*. In the span of five years he wrote bogus checks totaling $40,000, masqueraded as a Pan Am pilot to get free rides coast to coast, forged a Harvard University law diploma and got a job at the Louisiana state attorney's office. His most daring fraud came while impersonating a pediatrician in a Georgia hospital where he was the resident supervisor for the night shift. He covered his lack of medical knowledge by forcing his interns to do all the medical procedures. Through his elaborate frauds Abagnale gained fame, money and admiration.

It's interesting to note what type of lies Abagnale avoided. For instance, he never tried to pass himself off as a sex offender. Why? Because such a lie would have brought him isolation, ridicule and opposition. There would have been no advantage to telling such a lie.

If the first step of telling an effective lie is to try to gain some benefit, then what advantage did the disciples' lie get them? The following is a list of perks the disciples' lie brought them:

* James (son of Zebedee)—beheaded

* Philip—scourged, thrown in prison, crucified

* Matthew—slain with a crude half-axe, half-sword weapon called a halberd Andrew—crucified

* Mark—dragged to pieces

- Bartholomew—beaten and crucified

- Peter—crucified

- John—banished to the Isle of Patmos[2]

Seems crazy, doesn't it? Would you die for a lie that brought you nothing but ridicule, torture and death? To show how absurd this idea is, the early church historian Eusebius imagines the disciples gathering after Christ's death. One disciple tries to convince the others to lie about the resurrection. Eusebius envisions the speech sounding like this:

Let us band together to invent all the miracles and resurrection appearances which we never saw and let us carry the sham even to death! Why not die for nothing? Why dislike torture and whipping inflicted for no good reason? Let us go out to all nations and overthrow their institutions and denounce their gods! And even if we don't convince anybody, at least we'll have the satisfaction of drawing down on ourselves the punishment for our own deceit.[3]

How to tell an effective lie (part 2): Don't mention specific names or places. The disciples broke the cardinal rule of lying— don't mention specifics such as names or places. If your lie mentions actual people or places, then you've opened yourself up to being debunked. It's a lesson Marilee Jones learned the hard way.

DIGGING DEEPER
Not only did the disciples risk bodily harm for their lie; they also risked damnation. It may seem easy for us today to think about making up a new religion for gain. But to a first-century Jew, such an act was tantamount to lying against the God of Israel, as Paul himself argues in 1 Corinthians 15:12-19. Lying against God and perverting his revelation would mean risking the damnation of one's soul to hell. Would a person risk eternal torment for a few years of prestige as leader of a new religion? The answer can only be no.

BOGUS RÉSUMÉ AND JOSEPH OF ARIMATHEA'S TOMB

The Massachusetts Institute of Technology is arguably the best engineering school in the country, and getting in produces cut-throat competition. Ninety-two percent of the students applying have SAT math scores over 700. A key player in deciding who gets in is MIT's Dean of Admissions, Marilee Jones. She's extremely qualified to make such decisions since she herself has three earned degrees. Or so she said. In reality she was not even a college graduate.

Jones's biggest mistake was to put on her resumé degrees from three well-known universities. When administrators at MIT got suspicious all they had to do was to make three short phone calls. Two schools said they had never heard of her, while the third said she took a few classes but never graduated. Jones was busted. Despite earning MIT's highest award for administrators she was forced to resign.[4]

If the disciples' version of Jesus' resurrection is a lie, then they made the same mistake Jones made in being too specific with key details. In Mark's account of the burial of Jesus he states that Jesus was placed in the tomb of Joseph of Arimathea.[5]

> As evening approached, Joseph of Arimathea, a prominent member of the Council, who himself was waiting for the kingdom of God, went boldly to Pilate and asked for Jesus' body. . . . So Joseph bought some linen cloth, took down the body, wrapped it in the linen, and placed it in a tomb cut out of rock. (Mk 15:42-43, 46)

Do you see the problem?

The disciples, like Jones, violate the second step of telling a persuasive lie. Central to their lie is an actual person, Joseph of Arimathea.

Joseph was not just any person but a member of the Sanhedrin, which was a type of Jewish supreme court made up of seventy-one prominent men. If Joseph didn't have anything to do with Jesus' body, then he would have quickly contradicted their story, just as university administrators contradicted Jones's bogus resumé. Further, if Joseph did bury Jesus, then the location of his tomb would be known by all. Anyone desiring to check into the disciples' claim that Jesus rose from the dead could have simply walked over to the tomb and looked to see if Jesus' body was there or not. If the disciples were lying, then Jesus' body would still be in the tomb.

The apostles don't stop with Joseph of Arimathea. Paul weakens the lie even more when he claims that five hundred have come into personal contact with the risen Christ (1 Cor 15:6). He seems to be daring skeptics to track down these people and get their stories. Yet, if Christ's resurrection is a lie, then *none* of these five hundred people exists! Paul's bold claim will be quickly exposed.

How to tell an effective lie (part 3): Find a credible source to back your lie. A lie is more believable if you can convince someone to back your fib. When asking someone to back your story, however, make sure that person is cred-

DIGGING DEEPER

The graves of Jewish martyrs and holy men were carefully noted, cared for and honored. In fact, fifty such tombs in Jesus' day were sites of yearly veneration services in which people would gather to celebrate the life and teaching of the holy figure. Thus Jesus' tomb would have been carefully noted. Yet the early church never held veneration services at his grave—a fact that would have disgraced the name of Jesus, unless the earliest Christians did not think Jesus was there! Moreover, the church did venerate Jesus on a regular basis, but it was in acts of baptism and the Lord's Supper. What is odd is that it is not his person or teachings that are celebrated but his death—clearly a puzzling thing, unless the church believed his tomb was empty and he was raised!

ible. Ex-cons, prostitutes, drug dealers and known liars have little credibility, while nuns, police officers and teachers have high credibility. Having a person of low credibility vouch for your lie will only weaken it.

TO KILL A MOCKINGBIRD AND THE TESTIMONY OF WOMEN

In the 1962 classic film *To Kill a Mockingbird,* based on the 1960 book, Atticus Finch is a Depression-era attorney defending a black man accused of raping a white woman in the racist South. Since there are no witnesses to the alleged attack, it's a classic case of he said, she said. While Finch passionately defends a man he believes to be innocent, he's convinced the all-white jury will convict. Why? As an uneducated black man, the prisoner has no credibility with a racist jury. The twelve racist jurors will look at the skin of Finch's client and immediately suspect him of lying.

If the disciples were lying about Jesus rising from the dead, then they were wise to get others to support that lie. Choosing women as the first witnesses to the resurrection, however, was a fatal mistake. Women in first-century Palestine had even less credibility than Finch's client. Many first-century rabbis taught that it was better to burn the Law than teach it to a woman. One famous saying stated, "Blessed is he whose children are male, but woe to him whose children are female." A woman's testimony was viewed as worthless and could not be used in a Jewish court of law. Yet in the disciples' lie the first witnesses to the resurrection are women! As with Finch's client, the testimony of these women would have been viewed with extreme suspicion and prejudice. The only possible reason for the disciples to state that the first witnesses to the resurrection were women was because they actually were the first witnesses—an embarrassing fact the disciples would have to live with.

How to tell an effective lie (part 4): Anticipate pesky fact checkers! When telling a lie, make sure to carefully protect yourself from those desiring to expose you. All of us have people in our lives who (for whatever reason) want to see us fail and have the truth come to light. If you create a lie without considering how others may expose you, you are inviting failure. Just ask author James Frey.

A MILLION LITTLE LIES

James Frey was finding it difficult to get his novel about drug addiction, *A Million Little Pieces,* published. After multiple rejections, he converted his work of fiction into a memoir of his personal battle with addiction. With moving prose Frey describes for his readers a Novocain-free root canal, an alcohol-induced rage in which he runs down an Ohio police officer and brawls with responding officers, and his subsequent three-month stay in prison. Frey wrote that prison was a terrifying and sobering place.

Readers overwhelmingly resonated with his brutally honest account of addiction and transformation. "I think I wrote the events in the book truly and honestly and accurately," he told Oprah Winfrey during a television interview.[6] With Oprah's endorsement the book sold 3.5 million copies and sat on the *nonfiction* paperback bestseller list of the *New York Times* for fifteen weeks.

James Frey's ruse would have worked if not for a website called The Smoking Gun. This website exists to expose lies and embarrassing facts that those in the public spotlight want to keep hidden. After a six-week investigation, they discovered that most of Frey's outlandish claims were false. Court records show that Frey had not spent three months in jail but three hours for minor violations. The alcohol-induced rage and brawl with police officers—in which Frey claims he was charged with assault with a deadly weapon, assaulting an officer of the law, felony DUI and felony mayhem—

DIGGING DEEPER

The presence of women in the resurrection account was an embarrassment; this probably explains why the women are not mentioned in 1 Corinthians 15 and the speeches in Acts, since these speeches were evangelistic. There was no reason to include in evangelistic messages an incidental detail that would cause the audience to stumble and not deal with the main point. The fact is included in the Gospels because the Gospels are attempting to describe what actually happened. This point can be pressed home even more if we recall that one of the women, Mary Magdalene, had been possessed by demons (Lk 8:2)—a fact that would cast even more doubt on her veracity. It is no wonder that the disciples did not initially accept the women's report about Christ's resurrection: "They did not believe the women, because their words seemed to them like nonsense" (Lk 24:11).

could not be verified by *any* court documents. One prosecutor commented that "Felony Mayhem is not even an actual charge."[7]

Like Frey, the disciples faced their own investigative reporters. Those opposed to the disciples would have tracked down every outlandish claim made about Jesus' resurrection. There is one key difference between Frey's situation and the one the disciples faced. The reporters working at The Smoking Gun did not have anything personal against James Frey. Their job is to poke around for facts and see if everything checks out. If the paper trail leads nowhere, they move on to the next celebrity. The Jewish leaders, by contrast, had a vested interest in disproving the claims of the disciples. The resurrection story not only contradicted their deepest religious beliefs; it also weakened their social, religious and political power. They would have stopped at nothing to prove it false.

How to tell an effective lie (part 5): When the lie goes bad, save your own neck. Even if you carefully follow all the above steps, there is a chance your lie will be discovered. When things go bad, try to minimize the fallout by blaming others or providing misinformation. If possible, cut a deal that will save your neck and place the blame on others.

Law & Order

Debuting on September 13, 1990, *Law & Order* is the longest-running crime drama series on American television (six hundred episodes). Each episode begins with the now-famous introduction: "In the criminal justice system, the people are represented by two separate yet equally important groups: the police who investigate crime and the district attorneys who prosecute them. These are their stories."

Filmed on location in New York, the show is broken into two parts that tackle a crime from two different perspectives, that of the detectives and that of the prosecutors. In the first segment detectives track down leads and pursue suspects. In episodes involving multiple suspects there is always a crucial scene—interrogation of the suspects. How do you get a suspect to confess? How could you entice someone into sharing what he or she wants to keep hidden? The suspects are sent to separate rooms accompanied by a detective. Each detective says something like the following:

Here's how it works. If you tell us exactly what happened, we'll speak to the D.A. and try to cut a deal for you. This will go a lot better if you get in front of this and talk. Now, my partner is offering your pal the same deal in the next room. Whoever talks *first* gets the deal. It doesn't matter to me who gets it. Do you have anything to say?

In most episodes the suspect takes the deal and tries to pin the crime on his accomplice. The drive for self-preservation kicks in and a deal is made.

What's interesting about the disciples is that no one ever cut a deal. Not once, while facing torture, crucifixion or imprisonment, did a dis-

ciple turn on the others. No last-minute confessions or public decla-
rations denouncing the resurrection hoax. Would you be that committed to a lie gone bad? If offered a deal to spare your life or stop the
torture, wouldn't you renounce what you knew to be a lie and accept
a deal?

In the next chapter we'll consider the newest attack on the resurrection. It is a theory that has gained widespread acceptance and has
turned many away from a belief that Jesus rose from the dead.

The Resurrection

Conspiracy Theory or Fact? (Part 2)

From the Jesus Seminar to skeptical Bible professors who deny the resurrection, the current attack on the resurrection story asserts that what we have is mere legend. The premise is that Jesus was a caring social activist who wandered the countryside doing acts of kindness. His life was tragically cut short in his mid-thirties when he tangled with authorities. After his death, his followers understandably tried to keep his message alive by telling and retelling his story. The more they recounted his actions to others, the more Jesus took on divine qualities. Soon legend replaced fact. In the hearts of his followers Jesus went from being a social activist to being a miracle worker who not only claimed to be the Son of God but triumphantly conquered death by rising from the dead.

Makes sense, doesn't it? After all, haven't we all gotten carried away in our enthusiasm while telling a story and embellished it?

How should we respond to this disturbing claim about the core belief of our faith?

REASONS WHY THE LEGEND THEORY SHOULD BE REJECTED

In the following we discuss three lines of argument that show how the legend theory does not make sense of the facts. Each argument most likely will be the subject of its own conversation with a friend or coworker.

Argument 1: The biblical accounts of Jesus don't resemble legends. Legends are short on details, long on drama. Their characters are larger than life, act in dramatic ways and dominate the story. An effective way of showing that the Gospel accounts of the resurrection lack legendary features is to compare a legendary account of the resurrection with the biblical writers' account.

TALKING CROSSES AND MYSTERIOUS GIANTS

The following summary describes the so-called Gospel of Peter, written in the second century.

> In this account, the tomb is not only surrounded by Roman guards but also by all the Jewish Pharisees and elders, as well as a great multitude from all the surrounding countryside who have come to watch the resurrection. Suddenly, in the night there rings out a loud voice in heaven, and two men descend from heaven to the tomb. The stone over the door rolls back by itself, and they go into the tomb. Then three men come out of the tomb, two of them holding up a third man. The heads of the two men reach up into the clouds, but the head of the third man reaches up beyond the clouds. Then a cross comes out of the tomb, and a voice from heaven asks, "Have you preached to them that sleep?" And the cross answers, "Yes."[1]

This is how legends look. They are larger-than-life stories that lack details common to eyewitness accounts. Giant men whose heads reach to the clouds and a talking cross are the kinds of dramatic elements common to legends. These elements are precisely what are missing from the Gospel accounts.

In contrast to what you've just read, the Gospel accounts of the resurrection are filled with both relevant and irrelevant details. When reading John's account of the resurrection (Jn 20:1-8), we find an amazing amount of detail. In the first four verses John states:

> Early on the first day of the week, while it was still dark, Mary Magdalene went to the tomb and saw that the stone had been removed from the entrance. So she came running to Simon Peter and the other disciple, the one Jesus loved, and said, "They have taken the Lord out of the tomb, and we don't know where they have put him!"
>
> So Peter and the other disciple started for the tomb. Both were running, but the other disciple outran Peter and reached the tomb first.

From these verses we learn:

* The day of the week (first day)
* Time of day (while it was dark)
* Specific people involved (Mary Magdalene, Simon Peter, John)
* Peter coming in second in a race to the tomb.[2]

The Gospel writers put in seemingly irrelevant details because those details are part of what happened. In fact, the leaders of the Christian community go out of their way to assure early Christians that Christ's miracles and resurrection are not some type of myth or legend. Peter writes, "We did not follow cleverly invented stories when we told you about the power and coming of our Lord Jesus Christ, but we were eyewitnesses of his majesty" (2 Pet 1:16).

Argument 2: The Gospels contain embarrassing facts. When historians want to determine whether a particular document has been altered, they look for self-incriminating passages within the document. The thinking is that if a document sometimes casts the main characters in a negative light, then the writers had recording the truth, rather than protecting their subjects' image, as a central motive. Historical authors tend to leave out embarrassing details that would make the subject of their book look bad.

We often like our heroes to be larger than life, without fault or blemish. This has recently been demonstrated by two historians of the Alamo who have discovered that people don't want to know messy details about their legends.

THE ALAMO AND THE NEW TESTAMENT DOCUMENTS

The story of the Alamo is well known. Five thousand Mexicans surround the Alamo filled with 185 Texas freedom fighters led by James Bowie, William Travis and Davy Crockett. The Texans are surrounded but undaunted. When asked to surrender, Travis responds by shouting, "Victory or death!" In a series of fierce attacks Travis, Bowie, Crockett and all others die fighting bravely. Every Texan, regardless of age, fondly remembers the valor of the Alamo defenders.

But is that the whole story?

Two historians argue that making these men larger-than-life legends obscures their humanity. Rather than being men, they become cartoon characters.

In his book *How Did Davy Die?* historian Dan Kilgore argues that Crockett was taken alive from the Alamo and executed by a Mexican firing squad. Kilgore realizes he's messing with people's cherished idea of Crockett going down swinging his musket. People equate Crockett's being taken alive while all other defenders died during the siege as a sign of weakness and a character flaw. Kilgore has paid deeply for his opinion. He's received death threats and his books have to be kept under lock and key to keep them from being defaced.[1] Apparently the motto "Don't Mess with Texas" includes not messing with the state's heroes.

Jeff Long pushes even more buttons when he presents William Travis as a playboy with syphilis, Sam Houston as an alcoholic, and Jim Bowie as a man running away from debtors.[5] Long's views have also been violently attacked. It's not that these claims are new information to Texans; they just prefer them not to be made public. When the history of the Alamo is presented, most Texans prefer faultless heroes the size of their state.

No doubt the writers of the New Testament faced the same temptations as Texans. If the early Christians were, year after year, rewriting the history of their upstart movement, they certainly would be tempted to present themselves in the best possible light. They would present themselves as larger-than-life men who were turning the world upside down, resolute followers of Christ who didn't flinch in the face of danger. However, what we find in the Gospels are amazing examples of human faults and failures. Here's a partial list:

DIGGING DEEPER

First-century Jewish culture was an oral culture, that is, it preserved and passed on its important traditions largely through memorization and oral recitation in community gatherings. In such a culture, people had well-developed memorization skills and both the ability and concern to pass on unchanged reports of the words and deeds of important religious figures. Thus the facts about Jesus between A.D. 30, when he was crucified,[3] until the Gospels were written, that is, within the next two to six decades, would have been passed on and preserved in an oral context that would strengthen historical accuracy and make legendary development unlikely.

- One of the key leaders of the church, Peter, is called "Satan" by Jesus (Mk 8:33). To make matters worse, Peter is shown to deny Jesus three times after promising that he would never abandon him (Mt 26:33-35, 69-75).

- The disciples are presented as cowards who scatter when Christ is arrested and subsequently crucified.

- Mary Magdalene, Joanna, Mary the mother of James, and several other women find Jesus' tomb empty and report their finding to the mourning disciples, but the disciples think their words are an idle tale (Lk 24:1-11).

- When Jesus is distressed and needing their emotional support, the disciples fall asleep after being asked specifically by Christ to pray for him (Mk 14:32-41).

What's astonishing is that the Gospel writers even include potentially embarrassing details about the beloved founder of their movement. The most embarrassing fact about Jesus was his manner of death—crucifixion. To the Jews of the first century A.D., anyone being crucified was under God's curse (Deut 21:22-23). The Jews of Jesus' day were expecting the Messiah to be a conquering king who would triumph over Jewish enemies, not a crucified carpenter!

Now, if you were writing and rewriting the history of the Christian movement, wouldn't you weed out embarrassing details? The Gospel writers didn't remove these embarrassing facts, because they were not crafting a legend but writing history.

Argument 3: There was not enough time for legend to replace historical facts. Most people don't realize that one of the aspects about the Bible that is most frequently debated by scholars is when the books were written. The earliest Christian testimony consistently affirms that the Gospels, the book of Acts and the letters of Paul were all written relatively soon after the death of Christ. Why is this important? Because if these books and letters were written within two generations of the death of Christ, then it would have been impossible for legendary features to have crept into the biblical documents.

What's so special about the two-generation mark? A. N. Sherwin-White has argued that it takes at least two generations for legend to replace historical facts. In order for his conclusion to carry weight with a person, though, you must first establish Sherwin-White's credibility.

Sherwin-White was an Oxford historian and a member of the prestigious British Academy. The British Academy was established in 1902 and recognizes the finest scholarship in the humanities and social sciences. To get in you must prove that you are an expert in a particular field. In other words, you must write one or two books that establish you as an expert. Sherwin-White was an expert in Roman history. He wrote not just two books on the subject; he wrote six. In his most famous book, *Roman Society and Roman Law in the New Testament,* he establishes how long it takes for a legend to grow and replace facts. He claims that even two generations are often too short a time frame to allow legend to replace historical fact.

This is great news! If it can be shown that Matthew, Mark and Luke were written within two generations Christ's death, then according to A. N. Sherwin-White's expert opinion, it would be highly unlikely that they are legends. How would you go about dating these books? The key is deciding when the book of Acts was written. Why is dating Acts so important? Almost all scholars agree that Matthew, Mark and Luke (known as the synoptic Gospels) were written *before* Acts.[6] Therefore, these three books cannot be dated later than Acts.

DATING ACTS

Most conservative New Testament scholars argue that Acts was written around A.D. 60 to 62.[7] Oddly enough, this argument is mostly based on what Acts *doesn't* say. Luke, the accepted author of Acts, surprisingly does not mention two crucial events: the fall of Jerusalem and the death of the apostle Paul.

You can explain and illustrate how improbable these omissions are by presenting the following illustrations.

A SHORT HISTORY OF THE WORLD TRADE CENTER

Imagine you wanted to write a history of one of New York City's most recognized icon—the World Trade Center.[8] While the trade center consists of seven buildings, the most striking features are the twin towers, each consisting of 110 stories. You include the amazing fact that fifty thousand people work in the towers and over two hundred thousand visitors stop by each day. The towers are so huge that they warrant their own zip code: 10048. With that fact, your history ends.

If a person read your history, what would he or she conclude concerning when you wrote it? Obviously a reader would conclude it was written before September 11, 2001. Why? Your history makes no mention of the towers being destroyed when two hijacked planes slammed into them. It says nothing about the greatest act of terrorism our country has experienced or about the three thousand people who perished as a result. It would be unthinkable to write a history of the twin towers post 9/11 and not mention the destruction of the towers.

The same is true about the destruction of Jerusalem and the book of Acts.

Throughout the book of Acts, the author (Luke) is concerned with events that occur in Jerusalem. Every devout Jew views Jerusalem as the symbol of religious devotion and national pride. Above all, Jerusalem is the home of the temple.

Yet when Jerusalem falls to the Romans in A.D. 70, Luke does not mention it. Not once. Norman Geisler makes the point that the magnitude of the fall of Jerusalem far exceeds that of the destruction of the twin towers and the fatalities of 9/11. The Jews lost "their entire country, their capital city, and their temple, which had been the center of religious, political, and economic life for the last thousand years."[9] In the terrorist attacks of September 11, three thousand people were tragically killed. When Jerusalem was conquered, tens of thousands of Jews died. When Luke ends the book of Acts, Jerusalem and the temple are still standing.

The fact that the temple is still standing when Acts ends is of particular note because Luke passes up a golden opportunity to establish Jesus' credibility. In Luke's Gospel he records Jesus' controversial prophecy that Jerusalem would fall (Lk 21:20-24). Even more impressive is the fact that Luke (and Matthew) include the time frame within which this event would transpire—in Luke 21:32 Jesus prophesies that this would take place before a generation passes. Jesus likely died in A.D. 30. The destruction of Jerusalem in A.D. 70 is right on the mark. If Acts was written after the fall of Jerusalem, surely Luke would have highlighted Jesus' fulfilled prophecy.

One could also argue that Acts was written before Paul's death in A.D. 62. Why? In Acts Luke does not mention the death of one of the Christian community's key leaders, the apostle Paul. Point out to your friend how glaring this omission is by pointing to Lincoln's role in the American Civil War.

LINCOLN AND THE CIVIL WAR

In the musty back room of a museum you find an old pamphlet in a pile of Civil War documents. The pamphlet focuses on Abraham Lincoln's role in the American Civil War. The pamphlet begins with

Lincoln's inauguration on March 4, 1861. It covers Lincoln's reaction to the bloodiest battles of the war, including Shiloh, Antietam, Fredericksburg, Chancellorsville and Gettysburg. Special emphasis is given to his Gettysburg Address, which it describes as one of the most significant speeches in history. The pamphlet ends with Lincoln's last public address (April 11, 1865), in which he urges the nation to forgive and move forward.

After reading the pamphlet, when would you guess it was written? Obviously, the omission of Lincoln's assassination would strongly suggest it was written before April 14, 1865, when Lincoln was shot and killed in Ford's Theatre. No history of the Civil War would be complete without a detailed account of the first assassination of an American president.

DIGGING DEEPER

Paul wrote his epistles between A.D. 49 and 65. His view of Jesus is the same in his earliest letter (Galatians) as in his last letters (1 and 2 Timothy and Titus). Further, his view of Jesus is consistently supernatural—he knows of no merely charismatic social worker; he knows only of a miracle-working, incarnate Son of God who was bodily raised from the dead. This means that Paul had already come to accept a supernatural view of Jesus and his resurrection sometime before A.D. 49—sixteen years after Christ's death! But there's more.

The same is true of Luke's surprising omission of the death of Paul. Paul was the central leader of the young Christian community. Writing as a historian, Luke is careful to document when Paul is beaten, arrested and shipwrecked. In fact, half the book of Acts focuses on Paul. Yet when Acts ends Paul is alive and under house arrest. It's reasonable to assume that Luke doesn't record Paul's death in A.D. 62 because Acts was written *before* his death. This puts the date of Acts within thirty years of Jesus' death—well within Sherwin-White's minimum! This means that Luke's Gospel—the first of a two-set volume—was written before Acts, probably around

A.D. 58, or a mere twenty-eight years after the death of Christ.

EASTER FAITH: INSPIRATION OVER FACT

After listening to you speak about historical dates, legend versus fact and the veracity of the Gospel writers, your friend may suggest that none of what you've said really matters. To your friend the *story* of Jesus is more important to him or her than whether it's historically accurate. If the story of Jesus' struggles and triumphs provides one with hope, courage or a sense of forgiveness, then what does it matter if he was God or if he actually rose from the dead?

This is the view Oprah initially took with the James Frey book. When the facts of Frey's book were starting to be challenged, Oprah defended the spirit of the book. The "underlying message" of the book was that you could overcome addiction and redeem your life. What does it matter, Oprah argued, if some of the facts were embellished or false?[10]

Interesting idea, isn't it? Can a story, even if it's false, still bring you comfort or hope?

In various places Paul's letters include early hymns and creeds (1 Cor 15:3-8; Phil 2:6-11; Col 1:15-18; 1 Tim 3:16) that originated from and were used in church services in the early Jewish church in Jerusalem from A.D. 30 on. Many New Testament scholars believe these reflect the ideas of the earliest Jewish Aramaic-speaking believers at the time when they were beginning to gather in Jesus' name, to develop the core of their understanding of Jesus' identity, and to formulate their worship practices, recitations and songs. They also believe that this material was already in place and passed on to Paul early in his own development. All this implies a date around three to five years after Jesus' crucifixion. These various hymns and creeds in Paul's writings show that, within three to five years after Jesus' death, the early Jewish Christian community viewed Jesus as God incarnate and as one who rose from the dead.

THE TRUMAN SHOW

Truman (played by Jim Carrey) lives in the small town of Seahaven. He has a loving wife, devoted best friend and the support of his community. Every day is perfect. Life could not be any better for Truman if it were scripted. That's the problem. Unknown to Truman, Seahaven is a fictitious world created by television producers who are broadcasting Truman's life to the world twenty-four hours a day. His loving wife is an actress who secretly harbors disgust for him. His best friend says to Truman whatever the director, Christof, wants him to say. When Truman starts to suspect his world is not all it seems, his best friend assures him that his doubts are unfounded. "I would never lie to you," he says, repeating lines fed to him through his earpiece.

Truman's happiness, marriage and life are built on a lie. Yet what does it matter, if Truman is happy?

HARRY THE PHYSICS EXPERT

Harry is a hopelessly dumb physics student attending a large university. He fails all his first semester classes; his math skills are at a fifth-grade level; and he has no aptitude for science. One day all the physics students and professors at his college decide to fool Harry by making him think he is the best physics student at the university. Graders give him perfect scores on all assignments even though he deserves a failing grade. Eventually Harry graduates and goes on for a Ph.D., where the ruse continues. The professors at his university send a letter to all the physicists in the world and include them in the spoof. Harry receives his degree, takes a prestigious chair of physics, regularly delivers papers at major science conferences and is often featured in *Time* and *Newsweek*. He knows *nothing* about physics. Harry's life is full, with feelings of respect, accomplishment, expertise and happiness.

After presenting these illustrations, ask your friend whether he or she envies Harry or Truman. Does it matter that their lives are built on falsehoods? If you were in their shoes, would you want to know?

If Christ's bones are rotting somewhere under Palestinian dirt, then Christians are in the same situation as Truman and Harry. Our beliefs about our faith are false. Would Christians derive any comfort from a faith we know to be false? Our reaction would be the same as that of Truman, who, when finding out the truth, escapes Seahaven and searches for reality. Our reaction would be the same as Oprah, who, when finding out Frey's book is based on lies, no longer gleans courage from it. She renounces the book publicly on her show. Easter faith is *nothing* if the event Easter is based on never happened. Paul states it as forcefully as possible: "If Christ has not been raised, our preaching is useless and so is your faith" (1 Cor 15:14).

DIGGING DEEPER

We all know what a placebo is. It is an innocuous substance prescribed by doctors that does nothing to help an illness. But the patient's false belief that it works brings some mental relief. A placebo works due to naive, misinformed, false beliefs on the part of the patient.

Sadly, the placebo effect is not limited to medicine. Many people have worldview placebos—false, naive, misinformed beliefs that help them because they are living in a fantasy world of their own mental creation and not because of the truth of the beliefs themselves.

CONCLUSION

Could the entire Christian faith be based on a lie? Could the resurrection be an elaborate hoax started by the disciples and covered up by the church? Although the Gospels present him as a divine miracle worker, could Jesus really just be a common do-gooder turned into a larger-than-life legend? Claims like these bring a smile to conspiracy theorists. One Christian apologist, an expert on cover-ups, doesn't think these claims stand up to scrutiny.

WATERGATE AND A SHORT-LIVED LIE

Watergate was one of our nation's greatest political scandals and led to the resignation of Richard Nixon and the imprisonment of some of his top political aides. In order to protect the president from impeachment, some of his assistants tried to create and maintain a cover-up. It lasted only three weeks. Chuck Colson, one of Nixon's most trusted aides, explains: "The first to crack was John Dean. He went to prosecutors and offered to testify against the President. After that, everyone started scrambling to protect himself. . . . Some of the most powerful politicians in the world—and we couldn't keep a lie for more than three weeks."[11]

While in prison for his role in Watergate, Colson became a follower of Christ. What convinced him of the truth of Christianity? The implausibility of the disciples doing what he and Nixon's top aides couldn't do—successfully maintain a lie. These men had everything to gain by maintaining their silence. The disciples and earliest Christians apparently had nothing to gain by their silence—only persecution, marginalization and, in many cases, martyrdom. When Colson tries to persuade others of the veracity of the disciples' claims to have seen the risen Christ, he starts with Watergate. "The Watergate cover-up proves that twelve powerful men in modern America couldn't keep a lie—and that twelve powerless men two thousand years ago couldn't have been telling anything else *but* the truth."[12]

FURTHER READING

Bruce, F. F. *The New Testament Documents: Are They Reliable?* Downers Grove, Ill.: InterVarsity Press, 1981.

Craig, William Lane. *The Son Rises: The Historical Evidence for the Resurrection of Jesus.* Eugene, Ore.: Wipf & Stock, 2000.

McDowell, Josh. *More Than a Carpenter.* Wheaton, Ill.: Living Books, 2004.

8

What Would Machiavelli Do?

Ethics in a Morally Confused World

A banner hangs between two trees in your local park, stating, "It isn't *wrong* to think you're right, but it isn't *right* to think others are wrong." Nice sentiment, isn't it? It isn't wrong to have to personal convictions or opinions about what's right and wrong; it's just not right to judge the opinions of others. After all, what gives *you* the right say that another person's actions are wrong?

This modern attitude puts Christians in a difficult position. We believe that God sets the moral standard and that some things—fraud, premarital sex, cheating on your spouse, pornography, racism—are wrong for everyone. Today such a view is not popular and fosters some challenging questions:

- "What if we disagree about what's right and wrong?"

- "What gives you the right to force your views on me?"

- "Don't different cultures have different ideas of right and wrong?"

- "Can't I be good without God?"

While questions such as these can be challenging, they open the door for a rich conversation about morality, important social issues and God.

Since discussing morals and ethics can be a daunting task, we suggest you begin with a practical situation all of us are sure to encounter. Applying ethics to writing a résumé takes philosophical notions of right and wrong out of the classroom and puts it into the marketplace.

Your dream job becomes available. The night before the crucial interview, you sit down to polish your résumé. You remember reading on the Web that seven out of ten people embellish or lie on their résumés. Should you? Will your résumé be competitive if you don't? What ethical standard should guide you in your decision?

As you sit in front of your computer, you look over at two wristbands you've recently bought. Each has four letters imprinted on it. The first reads, "WWJD." This band reminds you that when writing your résumé you should ask the question "What would Jesus do?" The answer is obvious: being truthful is more important than advancing in your career. Jesus would strongly advise you *not* to lie on the résumé.

The second wristband, however, reminds you that Jesus is not the only option. It reads "WWMD" and would have you ask the question "What would Machiavelli do?" Machiavelli (1469–1527) was a political strategist who advocated deceit and manipulation in order to secure personal gain. He was ruthless in his pursuit of power and his name is synonymous with the phrase "The ends justify the means."

WHAT WOULD MACHIAVELLI DO?

In his bestselling book *What Would Machiavelli Do? The Ends Justify the Meanness*, Stanley Bing uses Machiavelli's insight to advise up-and-coming business leaders. One reviewer called it the "ultimate guide to corporate backstabbing." Bing's chapter headings reflect how Machiavelli would move up the corporate ladder.

• He would fire his own mother if necessary.

• He would be proud of his cruelty and see it as a strength.

• He would permanently cripple those who disappoint him.

• He would make you fear for your life.

• He would feast on other people's discord.

Machiavelli's view of lying is particularly helpful in writing your résumé. Bing elaborates: "The list of accomplished liars is long and impressive. It doesn't pay to name them all. It would, in fact, be easier to name those who did not lie when it became necessary, although that might be impossible. Those who do not lie do not succeed, and therefore remain unknown."[1] Machiavelli's advice concerning your résumé is clear: lie, lie, lie!

It's getting late and your résumé still isn't finished. How do you decide? Is it WWJD or WWMD?

It would be tempting to adopt whichever approach got you your dream job. What if you took the high road and wrote a truthful résumé, while someone following Machiavelli's strategy gets the job by writing a résumé filled with outlandish yet impressive lies? After learning you didn't get the job, you confront the person who lied. What do you do if the person disagrees with your assessment of his or her decision to lie? "Before you can disagree with anyone about anything," write Josh McDowell and Thomas Williams, "the two of you must agree on one thing: a standard of right and wrong."[2] Christians believe that only God can provide a standard for right and wrong that applies to all people. If he does not exist, then it's difficult to see how the teachings of Jesus are more ethical than the teachings of Machiavelli.

WHAT IS A MORAL ABSOLUTE?

When beginning to discuss morality with a friend, it's important to carefully define what you mean by a moral absolute. The existence of a moral absolute means there are some actions (racism, hatred, murder, oppression) that are wrong for everyone regardless of whether any person or culture believes them to be morally right. This definition rules out the notion that something might be true for one person but not for another. The basic idea is that we discover moral truths; we don't invent moral fictions. The key part of this definition that needs to be illustrated is that a moral absolute is binding regardless of whether a person believes in it or not.

MURDER ON A DESERTED ISLAND

Suppose you and one other person are shipwrecked on a deserted island. Year after year, it becomes painfully clear to both of you that you will never be rescued. Further, it occurs to you that if you were alone, all of the island's resources would be yours! There's no one—judge, police or priest—to remind you that murder is immoral. So you do it. Late at night, while the other survivor sleeps, you kill him or her. No witnesses. The perfect crime. Yet is murder still wrong if no one knows about it?[3]

GERMANY WINS!

In the *New York Times* bestseller *What If?* military historians imagine what might have been if history had been altered. What if the Americans had lost their war for independence? What if Lee had won at Gettysburg? What if D-day had failed? Historian John Keegan ponders a chilling question: What if Hitler had won?

Keegan argues that Hitler could have won WWII if he had thought more strategically about how he would meet his greatest need: oil. Without oil, his war machine was doomed to grind to a halt. Motivated by his hatred of Russia, Hitler decided to invade Russia and secure its enormous oil reserves. We now know that opening a two-front war was a fatal mistake. If, suggests Keegan, Hitler had first invaded Iraq, Iran and Saudi Arabia—the world's largest oil providers—he could have endlessly fueled his war machine. With oil secured, he could have taken his time defeating Britain and strategically mapped out an invasion of Russia. In the wake of such dramatic victories, the United States most likely would have allowed Hitler to conquer Europe.[4]

What if Hitler wasn't content to remain in Europe? What if his armies conquered not only the United States but the entire world? Hitler may then have systematically killed or brainwashed all who thought the Holocaust was wrong. Can you imagine a world where everyone thinks that murdering six million Jews is morally justified? Such a frightening world would bring up an interesting moral question: would the Holocaust still be wrong if everyone now thinks it's morally right? According to our definition, the answer is yes.

If your friend disagrees, point out the awkward position he or she has

DIGGING DEEPER

Moral relativists may not necessarily see a difference between the teachings of Machiavelli and those of Jesus. Moral relativism holds that everyone ought to act in accordance with his or her own society's code (or perhaps with the person's own individual code). What is right for one society is not necessarily right for another. For example, society A may have in its code "Lying on a résumé is morally permissible," while society B may have "Lying on a résumé is morally forbidden." In this case, lying is permissible for members of A and forbidden for those in B. Put differently, moral relativism implies that moral propositions are not simply true or false. Rather, the truth values (true or false) of moral principles themselves are relative to the beliefs of a given culture.

adopted. Is your friend saying that killing six million Jews would be morally justifiable if Hitler had won the war? Is killing a person on a desert island wrong only if someone else knows about it?

The next step in the conversation is to show that every person, to some degree, believes that certain actions are always wrong.

CREATING A "NOT TO BE TOLERATED LIST"

It's important to help a person create his or her own personal list of moral absolutes. We call this the Not to Be Tolerated List. This list consists of actions a person believes are wrong with no qualifications. You can help your friend create a Not to Be Tolerated List by presenting him or her with a list of moral actions and asking for judgment on whether each action is wrong. For example, most people would say that the torture of babies, the molesting of children, terrorism and racism are wrong. Philosophers Norman Geisler and Frank Turek argue that a person's belief in moral absolutes is revealed by his or her *r*eaction to certain moral acts.[5]

Instead of speaking in generalities, present these troubling situations and note your friend's reaction:

• Three Bosnian Serbs stand trial for creating and managing "rape factories" where Muslim women, some as young as twelve, endure unimaginable horrors. Victims tell of being savagely beaten, gang raped and tortured. The three Serbs state that they do not condone rape in general but argue that these particular women deserve it due to their ethnicity.[6]

- A mother in South Carolina secures her two children in their car seats and then drives the family car into a lake, drowning both. She tells authorities she did it to win back her boyfriend, who didn't want children.[7]

- The website Ku Klux Klan for Kids teaches young readers to be racists through cartoons, interactive games, puzzles and bedtime stories that portray people of color as inferior and dangerous. Creators of the website argue that they are merely doing what any good parent would do—passing on truth, values and convictions.

Situations such as these trigger what ethicist J. Budziszewsi calls a "baloney-meter." He explains, "Everyone carries around a personal baloney-meter in his mind. I'm speaking of the useful little instrument that lights up and beeps when you hear plain nonsense, prompting you to say to yourself, 'That's baloney.' "[8]

When we hear men try to justify the raping of women or explain why teaching children to be racist is good parenting, we view the act as immoral and the justification of it as baloney. Most of us, theists and nontheists alike, would agree that these acts are wrong regardless of whether a person thinks they are right. In other words, our belief that rape, the drowning of children and racism are wrong is binding whether a person believes it or not.

When creating your friend's Not to Be Tolerated List, consider the lists developed by the following noted thinkers.

ALAN DERSHOWITZ'S AWARENESS OF EVIL

Alan Dershowitz graduated first in his class from Yale University and at age twenty-eight was the youngest full professor at Harvard

Law School. He is a civil rights scholar who has defended Patty
Hearst, Mike Tyson and O. J. Simpson.

In a debate with Alan Keyes on whether religion can address today's problems, Dershowitz, a self-described agnostic, is asked,
"What makes something right?"

He responds that while it's difficult to say what is right, we
clearly know what's wrong. Dershowitz then shares his own Not to
Be Tolerated List with the audience.

> We know what absolute evil is. We've seen it. We've seen it
> in the name of secularism, Nazism. We've seen it in the
> name of atheism, Communism. We've seen it in the name
> of religion, the Inquisitions and the Crusades. We know
> what evil is. We know what wrong is . . .
>
> I DON'T KNOW WHAT'S RIGHT! I know what's
> WRONG.[9]

Dershowitz raises his voice because his baloney-meter is ringing.
Any attempt to justify the Holocaust, the Crusades or the Inquisitions
to him is ludicrous. Each of these acts is evil. Case closed.

AMNESTY INTERNATIONAL'S LIST OF ABSOLUTES

Amnesty International has 1.8 million members spread out over 150
countries. While these members come from divergent backgrounds
and nationalities, they are united in the effort to secure basic human
rights for everyone. This effort requires funding. In a letter asking for
donations, John Healy, executive director of Amnesty International,
shares his Not to Be Tolerated List with potential donors. "I am writing you today because I think you share my profound belief that *there
are indeed some moral absolutes.* When it comes to torture, to govern-
ment-sanctioned murder, to 'disappearances'—there are no lesser
evils. These are outrages against all of us."[10]

When hearing of the Holocaust or torture, we share Dershowitz's anger and Healy's belief in moral absolutes.

After helping your friend create his or her own Not to Be Tolerated List, communicate how much you agree with his or her list. Specifically point out all the ways your lists are similar. Finding points of agreement is important in creating a healthy dialogue.

Once these lines of agreement have been established, you can move to a part of your friend's list with which you differ.

The issue you want to discuss with your friend is what standard he or she is using to judge these acts to be immoral. The person believing in God believes rape is wrong because it violates God's moral standard. The person who does not believe God exists equally believes rape is wrong but must anchor that belief in something. If not God, then what?

In the next section we'll consider four different moral standards that our Not to Be Tolerated List could be rooted in.

POSSIBLE MORAL STANDARDS

When presenting these different op-

DIGGING DEEPER

When discussing moral absolutes, it is important to remain clear in understanding the issue before us. The question is not "Must we believe in God in order to live moral lives?" There is no reason to think that atheists and theists alike may not live what we normally characterize as good and decent lives. Similarly, the question is not "Can we formulate a system of ethics without reference to God?" If the nontheist grants that human beings do have objective value, then there is no reason to think he cannot work out a system of ethics with which the theist would also largely agree. Or again, the question is not "Can we recognize, say, that we should love our children?" Rather, as humanist philosopher Paul Kurtz puts it, "The central question about moral and ethical principles concerns their ontological foundation. If they are neither derived from God nor anchored in some transcendent ground, are they purely ephemeral?"[11]

tions, be careful not to present a weak version of the nontheist options. If we present a sloppy version of ethical anchors that exclude
God, our credibility will be greatly compromised when we present our
moral anchor.

Option 1: The powerful decide what is right. According to this position, those who hold power determine what is morally right. Justice
lies in the interests of the stronger party. When those in power are
honorable and compassionate individuals, then the interests of everyone are well looked after. Like King Arthur's fabled knights, those in
power commit to serve and protect the common person. According to
this option, if you find a wallet filled with cash and credit cards, you
look to the powerful to inform you about whether you have a right to
keep it. Arthur's knights would unequivocally command you to do the
honorable thing—return it.

Option 2: Morals are determined by culture. In this view individuals
follow the rules, values and norms of the culture in which they are
raised. Words such as *honor, fairness, beauty, commitment, evil, goodness* and *virtue* are defined for an individual by his or her own culture
and expressed in that particular culture's customs, laws and ethical
standards.

At the heart of this option is the idea of something like a social contract. In order to achieve a good life for the majority of people within
a particular culture, individuals agree on a list of social do's and don'ts.
Individuals within a society agree that you can't yell "Fire!" in a
crowded theater to get a better seat or ignore traffic signals to get to
work on time. If people regularly did, there would be chaos. We all
give up certain freedoms for mutual security and benefit. Morality,
then, is determined "not by some overarching absolute standard of
right and wrong but by the consensus of society. By common agreement, everyone accepts the morality expressed by the will of the majority."[12] In this view, returning a lost wallet all depends on the social

contract of your particular culture. If your culture adopts a "finders keepers, losers weepers" mentality, then the wallet is yours.

Option 3: Morals are determined by the individual. While all individuals are raised within a particular culture, it's up to the individual to decide what cultural do's and don'ts he or she will abide by. In this option a person is moral if he or she does what is right for him or her. With their conscience as a guide, individuals select what parts of the social contract they will follow, alter or ignore. This view requires a keen sense of discernment and introspection, often resulting in difficult ethical decisions. Will one person's self-interests be put over the interests of others? Keeping a lost wallet filled with cash is a decision only you can make. Do you need the money more than the owner? Either returning or keeping the wallet is permissible under this option.

Option 4: Morals are determined by a good God. In this option morality is rooted in God's unchangeable character. God determines what is right and wrong, and his commands reflect his goodness and holiness. "I, the LORD, speak the truth; I declare what is right," God proclaims in Isaiah 45:19. The Scriptures state that God is, among other things, wise (Is 28:29), holy (Ps 77:13; Is 6:3), loving (1 Jn 4:8) and good (Ps 100:5; 119:68). Thus all his commands are wise, holy, loving and good too. For example, because God is good, he commands that good should be done to *all* people (Gal 6:10). In fact, the key to living a moral life is to affirm what God calls good and oppose what he identifies as bad or evil. Under this option, finding another person's wallet would require you to return it to the owner. Why? Because a righteous God declares that dishonest gain is wrong (Ex 18:21; Ezek 22:13).

A TEST CASE: THE HOLOCAUST

When evaluating these four possible standards, it's useful to use a test case. A test case will allow your friend to judge the strengths and weaknesses of each option. One event that's sure to make a person's

DIGGING DEEPER

If moral standards reflect the commands of God so that murder is judged immoral because it violates God's commands, what if God changes his mind and starts commanding that murder is now permissible? Doesn't this show that the moral law is subject to change according to the whims of the Supreme Being?

Moral laws do not come from God's arbitrary commands, nor are they subject to the whims of a capricious Creator. The Christian God is not fickle and he does not change whimsically in his character and commands. These character defects may infect the Greek and Roman gods, but they do not exist within the Christian God. God's commands are based on and flow from his loving, good nature. These moral commands do not change, because God does not change (Mal 3:6). As James states, "Every good and perfect gift is from above, coming down from the Father of the heavenly lights, who does not change like shifting shadows" (Jas 1:17).

Not to Be Tolerated List is the Jewish Holocaust. Movies such as *Schindler's List* graphically remind us of the horrors of Hitler's final solution. The extinction of more than six million Jews stirs in us powerful emotions and moral outrage. Yet by what standard do we judge the Nazis' actions as wrong?

At first that seems like a silly question. "Of course the Holocaust is wrong," says your friend. We agree. Yet what standard allows us to condemn the Holocaust with the full conviction we feel?

With the Holocaust as a test case, move through the four options and see which option allows us to condemn what we know to be wrong. Your friend may be surprised by the results.

Option 1: The powerful decide what is right. When the powerful are fair and honorable, like Arthur's knights, this option results in an ethical society. But what if those who have the power are the Nazis?

In 1933, when Hitler came to power, he dissolved all political parties other than his own. The National Socialists dismissed all judges and lawyers of Jewish descent and appointed new ones. They allowed only those of pure German heritage behind the bench. Thus, far from acting outside the laws of his land, Hitler acted in accordance with Germany's laws. He had full power to determine what was right and wrong. Six million Jews and five million gypsies and homosexuals would soon experience the wrath of that power.[13]

While we may condemn Hitler's actions, we can't deny that he technically had the authority to do it.

Option 2: Morals are determined by culture. In his book *Morality After Auschwitz,* Peter Haas argues that the German culture of the 1930s and 1940s embraced an ethic that paved the way for Hitler's final solution. Richard Rubenstein, in his review of the book, summarizes Haas's view: "The Holocaust as a sustained effort was possible only because 'a new ethic was in place that did not define the arrest and deportation of Jews as wrong and in fact defined it as ethically tolerable or even good.' "[14] Do you see the problem? If the Germans were merely following a German social contract, then how can we say that what they did was wrong? What gives the creators of one social contract the right to judge the social contract of another culture?

Option 3: Morals are determined by the individual. The Holocaust was Hitler's personal vision to rid Germany of one of its greatest internal threats: the Jews. Even if it could be argued that most of the citizens of Germany opposed the death camps, it was Hitler's conviction that the camps were morally and logically justifiable—a conviction he chillingly describes in *Mein Kampf* (1924):

> If nature does not wish that weaker individuals should mate with the stronger, she wishes even less that a superior race should intermingle with an inferior one; because in such cases all her efforts, throughout hundreds of thousands of years, to establish an evolutionary higher stage of being, may thus be rendered futile.[15]

For Hitler, what was best for him and the German people was the extermination of the inferior Jews. If morals are determined by the individual, then how can Hitler's actions be wrong for him?

Each of the above standards fails to allow your friend to condemn what he or she knows to be wrong. The one thing sure to make everyone's Not to Be Tolerated List must be taken off.

The predicament your friend finds himself or herself in is the same moral quandary the prosecution stumbled into when trying to prosecute the Nazis after the war. Just as your friend knows the Holocaust is wrong, so the Allied Forces knew it was wrong and wanted to punish the Nazi leaders. Yet what standard would they use? This question would be turn out to be surprisingly difficult to answer.

THE LAW ABOVE THE LAW

The Nuremberg trials were a series of court cases (1945–1949) held in Nuremberg, Germany, prosecuting leaders involved in the Nazi regime. The most famous trial involved twenty-four key Nazi leaders charged with crimes against humanity.

Individuals following the trial were shocked at how effective the Nazis' defense team was in arguing against the charges. How is that possible? What defense could be given for the indefensible? "The most telling defense offered by the accused was that they had simply followed orders or made decisions within the framework of their own legal system, in complete consistency with it, and that they therefore could not rightly be condemned because they deviated from the alien value system of their conquerors."[16]

A strong argument, isn't it? The Nazis' lawyers were simply appealing to a moral standard we've already considered. If morals are determined by culture, then how can you convict Germans for following the values, laws and beliefs of German culture? If the Germans had won the war, there wouldn't even be a trial.

> The trial came to a halt.
>
> How would the prosecution respond? The chief counsel of the United States, Robert Jackson, came up with an answer. The only way to judge any culture, he argued, was to appeal to a "law above the law." A "law above the law" transcends culture and applies to both the winners and losers of the war. The trial continued and justice was served.

While he didn't state it directly, what Jackson appealed to was the only option that allows us to keep the Holocaust on our Not to Be Tolerated List.

Option 4: A good God sets the moral standard. To murder anyone, Jews or Germans, is wrong because of God's command "You shall not murder" (Ex 20:13). God deems murder wrong because all people have been created by him and bear his image (Gen 1–3). All people, regardless of ethnicity, are beings loved by God. Not to judge murder as evil would violate notions of justice, compassion and love rooted in God's character and found in our moral intuition. God's moral decrees are binding on all people at all times. As someone once quipped, when Moses came down from Sinai, he didn't bring with him the Ten Suggestions.

Only this last option—God sets the moral standard—provides the foundation to fully denounce Hitler's brutality and keep the Holocaust on your Not to Be Tolerated List.

In the next chapter we'll offer evidence why there exists a Not to Be Tolerated List that applies to all of us.

What Would Machiavelli Do? (Part 2)

Men raping women based on their ethnicity. A mother drowning her children to win back a boyfriend. An interactive website that teaches kids to be racist. According to Os Guinness, an appropriate response to such atrocities is to exclaim, "Goddammit." He writes:

> Absolute evil calls for absolute judgment. Instinctively and intuitively, we cry out for the unconditional to condemn evil unconditionally. The atheist who lets fly "Goddammit!" in the face of evil is right, not wrong. It is a signal of transcendence, a pointer toward a better possibility—and unwittingly a prayer.[1]

We condemn certain actions because we intuitively know they are wrong. Yet where does our intuition come from? Is the moral intuition we feel common to all people? What evidence can we muster to prove moral intuition?

ARGUING FOR MORAL INTUITION

The Not to Be Tolerated List described in the last chapter is a powerful example of the intuitive argument for the existence of moral absolutes. We instinctively know that it's wrong to drown your kids because they've become a nuisance. To say that something is intuitive is to argue that you have direct awareness of it. It's not a hunch but a way of perceiving something and knowing it's true. "Intuitional truth," write Francis Beckwith and Gregory Koukl, "is simply known by the process of introspection and immediate awareness."[2] In other words, there are some truths you don't need to be taught or have proved to you—they are obvious and serve as the building blocks for all other knowledge.

WHO'S TALLER?

What if you presented a friend with the following riddle: "If John is taller than Mary, and Tom is taller than John, is Tom taller than Mary?"[3] You tell your friend that you know the riddle is difficult, so he or she can take as much time as necessary. You tell your friend that if he or she is stuck, you can even bring all three out—John, Mary and Tom—so you can put them next to each other and determine the answer. Your friend looks at you and laughs. "No, that won't be necessary," your friend responds. "Tom is taller than Mary," he or she says quickly, losing interest.

The thinking process your friend used to determine that Tom is taller than Mary is intuitive. A study of formal logic is not necessary. It just makes sense that Tom is taller than Mary based on Tom's relation to John.

DOES IRELAND EXIST?

What if a person said to you, "Ireland exists and has wonderful pubs and citizens" and then in the next breath declared, "Ireland does not exist and thus has no pubs or citizens"? You would not need to consult a map or book a flight to Ireland to know those statements can't both be true. You don't need an advanced degree in philosophy to understand that the claims are mutually exclusive. Either Ireland exists or it doesn't; both claims can't be true.

What can be said about our thinking process concerning Tom and Mary or our intuitive awareness of exclusive claims can be said about morals. Think back to the acts recorded on your Not to Be Tolerated List. A person does not need to make an argument for why rape, the drowning of children and racism are wrong. We just know they are!

GLOBAL MORAL INTUITION

The writings of C. S. Lewis powerfully strengthen the argument for moral intuition. When we look at civilizations as a whole, notes Lewis, we observe that almost all cultures, past and present, surprisingly have the same moral intuition. Each of these divergent cultures "had an idea that they ought to behave in a certain way."[4] Lewis is arguing against the popular idea that different civilizations and different ages have had radically different moralities. "If anyone will take the trouble to compare the moral teaching of, say, the ancient Egyptians, Babylonians, Hindus, Chinese, Greeks and Romans, what will really strike him will be how very alike they are to each other and to our own."[5]

It's crucial to note that these diverse cultures had little or no contact with each other. They were not placing international phone calls and comparing moral codes or reworking their lists to cultivate consensus. Yet consensus is exactly what appears when we compare their lists. It's as if a billion musicians, in thousands of different locations, were playing off the same sheet of music.

To illustrate your point, ask your friend the following: "What would it look like if a country created a radically different set of moral codes?" Try to create with your friend an imaginary country whose morals are contradictory to universally acknowledged morals.

An Unimaginable Country

Write down the opposite of the following traits:

Honesty:

Bravery:

Respect:

Love:

Kindness:

In our make-believe country parents intentionally teach their children to lie, be cowards, disrespect adults, hate and be cruel to everyone.

It's hard to imagine, isn't it?

The Christian argues that the moral similarities across cultures are due to God's placing a specific idea of right and wrong into the hearts of men and women regardless of geographic location. While different cultures may express the idea through different customs, they are working off the same page, morally. It is a moral idea that haunts every culture.

Two Objections

After you've presented the preceding illustrations, be prepared for some questions from your friend or family member. Here are two possible objections to the argument you've presented.

First objection. What about the unseemly side of this global intuition? You conveniently note the positive qualities—truthfulness, mercy, compassion—that are common to cultures yet leave out the negative ones, such as war, oppression and violence. Yes, most cultures consistently promote kindness as a virtue, but then they consistently engage in acts of violence. The *Encyclopedia of Military History* contains over a thousand pages that graphically record acts of violence between cultures and countries. "The defining feature of humanity," states one historian, "is inhumanity."[6]

So, did God plant *both* mercy and violence into our cultural consciousness?

Two responses are in order. First, it's interesting to note that when we bring up negative aspects of human conduct such as war, we intuitively label them as "dark" or "unseemly." We recognize that just as cultures do things that are noble, so they also do things that are regrettable. Where did that distinction come from? "A man does not call a line crooked," notes Lewis, "unless he has some idea of a straight line."[7] To recognize that certain cultures periodically stray from the moral norm is to acknowledge that a moral norm exists.

Second, our sense of moral intuition is not automatically binding. In our chapter discussing the problem of evil, we noted that the greatest compliment God gave us is that he didn't make us into Mr. or Mrs. Wonderful Dolls who robotically obey him. Tragically, we can disregard our moral intuition and, over time, mute it. What's interesting to note is that when we do choose to go against our moral intuition, we are often acutely aware of it.

MUNICH

Steven Spielberg's film *Munich* recreates the kidnap and murder of eleven Israeli athletes during the 1972 Munich Olympics. The world is in shock as word comes that all eleven athletes perished during a failed rescue attempt. How will Israel respond?

In a pivotal scene Prime Minister Golda Meir elects not to bring the Palestinians to formal justice. Instead, she secretly forms an Israeli death squad who systematically hunt down and assassinate eleven Palestinian suspects. The assassins are paid under the table, travel with assumed names and carry false passports.

Why the secrecy? Because Meir, in her heart, knows she is doing wrong. The right course of action would be to capture the suspects and prosecute them in an Israeli court of law. But she opts for revenge. She explains, "Every civilization finds it necessary to negotiate compromises with its own values."

While Meir compromises Jewish values and seeks revenge, she is conscious of making a compromise. She knows what's right, even as she chooses violence over justice. The history of human culture is filled with similar conscious compromises. We are fully aware when our line goes crooked.

Second objection. While your friend may acknowledge the common moral thread running through cultures, he or she may offer a different explanation for it—evolution. Isn't it possible that different cultures created similar moral codes because humans evolved roughly at the same rate? Morals are merely instincts needed to survive, and through evolution, humans eventually found themselves on the same page, morally.

"It is conceivable," states Christian philosopher C. Stephen Evans, "that evolution could be used to explain various instincts or social feelings." He explains, however, that our deep sense of morality does not seem to be merely one more instinct. "It is not an instinct, because it is itself the standard by which we judge our instincts to be good or bad."[8]

WHEN INSTINCTS CRASH INTO EACH OTHER

The movie *Crash* won the Oscar for best picture (2005) for provocatively showing the foundations of racism and misunderstanding. In one scene a racist white police officer (Matt Dillon) pulls over an African American couple and proceeds to administer a field sobriety test to the husband. When the wife steps out of the car to complain, the officer forces her against the car and fondles her during a search. As he sexually harasses her, he dares the husband to stop him. Dillon's partner is so disgusted by the event that he requests a transfer to a different squad car.

The next day, Dillon arrives at the scene of an overturned car on the highway. The car is crushed, leaking gas and about to burst into flames. He crawls inside to help the pinned driver. When the two make eye contact, he recognizes the driver as the woman he harassed the night before. Recognizing him, she screams, "Don't touch me!" Officers yell for him to get out of the car before it blows. Imagine the powerful instincts the officer is experiencing. The instinct of survival tells him to get out of danger. The instinct of preservation tells him it would be better if she died, thus ensuring that no charges will ever be filed against him. Yet the instinct to save this woman seems stronger. Why? Because it's what he *ought* to do. Risking death and prosecution, he drags her from the car. Evolution is powerless to explain a moral *ought* that trumps other instincts.

REJECTING MORAL ABSOLUTES

The last step in the conversation is to help a person realize what it means to reject the argument we've been making. If a person rejects the idea of moral absolutes, then he or she needs to wrestle with the negative implications of that rejection.

Let's consider two implications.

First, rejecting moral absolutes makes activism impossible. "A rich life," writes Cornel West, "is trying to leave the world a little better than you found it."[9] Most of us would agree with West's assessment. However, as soon as we try to make the world a better place, we run into significant philosophical difficulties. Make the world better according to whose standards? Do you see the dilemma? We want to make the world a better place, but what gives us the right to do it?

IS A LAW JUST?

Sitting in his Birmingham jail cell, Martin Luther King Jr. grew increasingly angry. He thought of the pain he saw in his daughter's face when he had to tell her that the new amusement park, Funtown, was closed to colored children. He thought of his family sleeping in a car because the "whites only" motels refused his family lodging. He knew the laws that made segregation a reality were wrong, but what gave him the right to challenge them? If morality is determined by a culture's social contract, then it would be unethical for King to challenge the racist laws of Alabama. Yet King did challenge the laws of the land.

In his now-famous "Letter from Birmingham Jail," he explained what fueled his activism. "A just law," wrote King, "is a man-made code that squares with the moral law of God. An unjust law is a code that is out of harmony with the moral law." King closed his letter by hoping "that the dark clouds of racial prejudice will soon pass away" and be replaced with the "radiant stars of love and brotherhood."[10]

DIGGING DEEPER

The objective moral order contains imperatives about what ought and ought not to be the case—for example, "Do not murder" and "Pursue honesty." Atheists can account for descriptions only of what is the case, not of what ought to be the case. You cannot get an ought from a mere is. From the fact that something is the case (people do practice lying or honesty), it does not follow that it ought or ought not be the case.

If the universe begins with a big bang and mere matter, as scientific atheists claim, then reality will merely consist in what is the case, not in oughts. By contrast, we all know where an ought or imperative comes from—a person with a will. A good imperative comes from a good person with a will. Thus the "law above the law" is best explained as having been willed by a good, loving Person.

King's activism, rooted in a belief in moral absolutes, was instrumental in repealing Alabama's laws. Without a belief in God's moral law, his activism would have been unjustified.

Second, rejecting moral absolutes mutes our moral outrage. Moral outrage is stoked by the belief that some actions, regardless of a person or culture's reasoning, are evil. Some actions simply shouldn't be tolerated.

THE LOTTERY

In Shirley Jackson's short story "The Lottery" townspeople meet once a year to participate in a shocking ritual. They meet to select and kill one person from their community. That person serves as a human sacrifice to ensure a profitable crop. The person to be sacrificed is selected through a lottery.

Jackson graphically describes a woman who selects a piece of paper with a black dot. Even though she is a wife and mother, she is to be sacrificed. "It isn't fair, it isn't right," she pleads. Her cries fall on deaf ears. The townspeople, including her husband and children, pick up stones. She is crushed in a hail of rocks. The townspeople leave her crumpled body to tend to the crops.

When the story was first released in 1948, the publisher was deluged with letters denouncing it. In a post-Hitler era, people were angered by the savage killing of an innocent victim.

Times have seemingly changed.

The change was noticed by Kay Haugaard, a literature professor in southern California who has taught creative writing since the 1970s. When she first used "The Lottery" as a writing sample, her students were outraged at the thought of human sacrifice. However, she's noticed a slow decline in her student's outrage. One class shocked Professor Haugaard by having *no* reaction.

"The ending was neat!" commented one student. "It's their ritual," offered another. After Haugaard shared her personal opposition to the act, one student responded, "Well, I teach a course for our hospital personnel in multicultural understanding, and if it's part of a person's culture, we are taught not to judge, and if it has worked for them . . ."

Haugaard sat stunned. She reports in *The Chronicle of Higher Education*, "No one in the whole class of more than twenty ostensibly intelligent individuals would go out on a limb and take a stand against human sacrifice."[11]

For moral outrage to exist, it must be fueled by the belief that some things—racism, terrorism, sexism, human sacrifice—are morally reprehensible. Yet without a moral standard that exists above this farming community's ritual, how can we judge or oppose their custom?

CONCLUSION

A new job opens. It's time for you to submit another résumé. Will you write it in the spirit of Jesus or the spirit of Machiavelli?

If morals are determined by the individual, then you are free to choose. Be warned, though. If you choose Machia-

DIGGING DEEPER

Moral relativism suffers from a problem known as the reformer's dilemma. If relativism is true, then it is logically impossible for a society to have a virtuous, moral reformer like Jesus Christ or Gandhi. Why? Because moral reformers are members of a society who stand outside that society's code and pronounce a need for reform and change in that code. However, if an act is right if and only if it is in keeping with a given society's code, then the moral reformer himself is by definition an immoral person, for his views are at odds with those of society. Moral reformers must always be wrong because they go against the code of their society. But any view that implies that moral reformers are impossible is defective because we all know that moral reformers have actually existed!

velli, you must do one thing first—kill your conscience. "The eradication of conscience," writes Stanley Bing, "is one of the toughest things you're going to have to learn." To be a real Machiavellian is to disregard any notions of God or transcendent responsibilities and act like an infant who cares only about himself or herself. Bing concludes, "You, too, can eliminate your conscience by finding the inner infant within you and hauling it into the daylight. As you grow younger and younger, you will find the part of you that punishes yourself for bad behavior disappearing. Man, does that feel good! And how free you will be to do anything."[12]

For Hitler, the freedom to do anything included the mass murder of those he thought inferior. For the townspeople in "The Lottery," the freedom to do anything meant joining in human sacrifice. Unfortunately for you, the eradication of conscience means that the person with whom you are competing for a job may feel free to pad a résumé with lies. After all, that's what Machiavelli would do.

Christians believe that the conscience, when in line with God's moral law, is a key part of what it means to be made in the image of God. It is the voice within us that defines what's right and wrong and spurs us on to pursue justice and oppose evil.

FURTHER READING

Beckwith, Francis, and Gregory Koukl. *Relativism: Feet Firmly Planted in Mid-Air.* Grand Rapids: Baker, 1998.

Budziszewski, J. *The Revenge of Conscience: Politics and the Fall of Man.* Dallas: Spence, 1999.

Lewis, C. S. *The Abolition of Man.* New York: Macmillan, 1986.

Rae, Scott. *Moral Choices: An Introduction to Ethics.* 2nd ed. Grand Rapids: Zondervan, 2000.

10

Are We an Accident?

Arguing for God Through Design

Human eyes are composed of more than two million working parts and can, under the right conditions, discern the light of a candle at a distance of fourteen miles.

The human ear can discriminate among some four hundred thousand different sounds within a span of about ten octaves and can make the subtle distinction between music played by a violin and that played by a viola.

The human heart pumps roughly a million barrels of blood during a normal lifetime—a quantity that would fill more than three supertankers.

What are to make of these facts?

If you believe in God, these facts confirm what is obvious—we are the handiwork of a wise Designer. You join the psalmist in declaring that we are all "fearfully and wonderfully made" (Ps 139:14).

Others read these same facts and attribute our amazing bodies to billions of years of evolutionary refinement. To them, a belief in God is a naive attempt to replace science with faith.

The intensity of this disagreement has spilled over into our courts and school curriculums. *Time* magazine reflected this disagreement in a cover story appropriately called "The Evolution Wars."[1]

How can we present our deep conviction that we and the world we live in are powerful examples of God's design?

THE ARGUMENT FROM DESIGN

The argument from design is a favorite because it rests on three commonsense ideas: First, where there is design, there is a designer. Second, signs of design are obvious in our bodies and in the world around us. Third, the design we see in ourselves and in the world should be attributed to an intelligent Designer.

When presented with evidences of design in our bodies, a sunrise, a fetus growing in the womb, or our galaxy, we can conclude that they are mere coincidences or unexplainable scientific facts. Or we can explain them with the same commonsense approach we use to explain examples of design in a computer, a camera, or a painting—they are the product of an intelligent mind.

Since the concept of design is crucial to the argument you are about to make, it is important to define what you mean by design. Consider starting the conversation by asking, "What does it mean to say that something has been designed?" Suggest to your friend that design is present when something shows evidence of forethought, planning and intention.

MOUNT RUSHMORE

You and your friend are hiking in the Black Hills of South Dakota. As you round a hill, you come upon a sight that stops you in your tracks. In front of you are four giant faces carved into stone. Each head is as tall as a six-story building. The faces are a perfect likeness of four American presidents—Washington, Jefferson, Teddy Roosevelt and Lincoln.

After taking photos of this magnificent find, what conclusions would you come to concerning its origin? How did these faces appear on this mountainside? What reasonable options are there to explain it?

Perhaps they happened through chance. Over the years, wind and rock slides combined to produce these four faces. But that seems silly, doesn't it? We know that Mount Rushmore exhibits the three signs of design: forethought, planning and intention.

Mount Rushmore is the brainchild of sculptor John Gutzon Borglum. Borglum wanted to create a memorial of America's most revered presidents (intention). Borglum and his four hundred workers devised an ingenious method of removing more than eight hundred million pounds of stone created by the blasting (planning). Before the blasting could begin, designers mapped out the size and shape of each president. The presidents' noses are twenty feet long and rest above mouths that are eighteen feet wide. Each of the presidents' eyes is eleven feet across. The carvings are scaled to individuals who would stand 465 feet tall (forethought). After fourteen years of work, the four busts were completed and Mount Rushmore opened to the public in 1941.

The key transition Christians make while presenting the argument from design is that the same intention, planning and forethought found in man-made creations like Mount Rushmore are found in the complexity of the human body. Just as we attribute the design of Mount Rushmore to the work of John Gutzon Borglum, so we ought to attribute the design found in our bodies to the handiwork of God.

This line of thinking was perfected by William Paley in the 1800s. Paley wrote several influential books on Christianity and philosophy and his works were required reading at Cambridge until the twentieth century. He believed that God had intricately designed the human body, yet he struggled to find a way to communicate his conviction to his skeptical friends. It was obvious to Paley that just as a master craftsman carefully assembles a watch, table or telescope, so God crafts the human body.

THE HUMAN EYE COMPARED TO A TELESCOPE

Paley came up with an idea: why not list for his friends the similarities between something a craftsman makes and something God makes? He chose a telescope and the human eye. After Paley finished his study of the eye, he presented to his friends a list of similarities between it and a high-powered telescope.

- The eye was made for vision; the telescope was made for assisting it.
- Each uses a sophisticated lens to achieve its function and purpose.
- Both reflect and manipulate light.
- Both are able to bring an object into proper focus. The muscles surrounding the soft lens of the eye move to bring objects into focus, while a telescope uses dials to move the lens.[2]

After Paley showed his list to his friends, he had them consider if it would be reasonable to believe that the telescope was created by a craftsman while the eye was not. This is the same question you may want to present to your friend or coworker. If a telescope and the human eye both display evidence of planning, forethought and intention, then shouldn't both be considered products of design? If the answer is yes, then common sense tells us that where there is design there is a Designer.

While the conclusion Paley draws from comparing a telescope to a human eye (both are the work of a creative mind) is convincing to you, be prepared for what could be a major detour in the conversation. The objection of evolution is a serious challenge to the argument you've been making during this particular conversation.

THE OBJECTION OF EVOLUTION

Your friend may share Paley's admiration for the eye but have a different explanation for its design. After millions of years of evolution and refining, the human eye *should be* complex and awe-inspiring. Without this crucial organ, the human animal would never have survived.

How should you respond?

We suggest that you consider using one or two different responses. Each response tackles the difficult issue of evolution in a different way.

Response 1: Lincoln's approach. Abraham Lincoln once stated that in a debate he would concede all points to his opponent except the most important. Lincoln's strategy often unsettled his debating adversaries. In the spirit of Lincoln, Christian philosopher C. Stephen Evans

DIGGING DEEPER

Regardless of how one presents the argument from design, at the heart of the argument is the concept of design. Throughout history a number of kinds of design have been used by advocates of the design argument.

• *Design as order: From spatial arrangements of the parts of the human eye to towns with organized streets at right angles to each other our universe is filled with orderliness.*

• *Design as purpose: A watch is a complex whole consisting of several parts that interact to achieve an end, namely recording the time. This arrangement of parts reflects a plan in the mind of the watch's designer.*

• *Design as simplicity: Movements as diverse as an apple falling and a galaxy rotating can be explained by the simple laws of motion expressed by Isaac Newton. But why should the world be simple? Why should it be a unity? The fact that the world exhibits unity and simplicity is taken* as evidence that behind it stands a Designer who made it in a simple, efficient, unified way.

- Design as complexity: The organic compounds in living organisms come in four groups: carbohydrates, lipids, proteins and nucleic acids. These compounds exhibit a staggering complexity in their composition as well as a precise intricacy in their relationships with each other. When one realizes that the world exhibits such complexity, and that at the same time this complexity can be expressed in simple terms, then this can be seen as evidence of an intelligent Designer.

Viewing design as order, purpose, complexity and simplicity gives the design argument a force and power that can be appreciated only through a detailed presentation of each one.

If looking at Mount Rushmore causes you to acknowledge the work of sculptors, then why shouldn't the complexity of our bodies cause us to consider an intelligent Creator?

concedes, for the sake of argument, that evolution is true. Evans's point is both unexpected and persuasive. He simply states that evolution is not logically incompatible with the argument from design or the existence of God. Why does it matter, states Evans, if God accomplished creation either through a command or through an "intricate and elegant set of orderly natural processes" known as evolution?[3] Even if evolution is true, the order and design found in it still need explanation. As long as the indicators of design are present, it doesn't matter whether the object was made quickly or slowly or which steps the designer took to do his work. We are still justified in identifying it as the product of intelligence.

The strength of this response is that it may disarm a significant part of your friend's objection. Your friend may expect you to be defensive at the mere mention of evolution. Communication experts Roger Fisher and William Ury suggest that individuals should regularly look for ways to act inconsistently with perceptions. They write, "Perhaps the best way to change their perception is to send them a message different from what they expect."[4] The message you are sending is that evolution, if proved true, would not necessarily entail your having to abandon God. Evolution is a theory that needs to account for the intricate design inherent in it. If God isn't the source of this design, then what is?

Response 2: Using Darwin's criteria to judge evolution. This second response focuses on why many people, Christians and non-Christians alike, question the validity of evolution. As a scientist, Darwin knew that any theory must have clear criteria of what would support or discredit the theory. Darwin laid out his criteria for evolution in *On the Origin of Species:* "If it could be demonstrated that any complex organ existed which could not possibly have been formed by numerous, successive, slight modifications, my theory would absolutely break down."[5]

While Darwin's candor is notable, he was quickly challenged by biologists who pointed toward an organ we've already considered in this chapter—the eye. Indeed, the eye would come to haunt Darwin. Michael Behe, a defender of intelligent design, explains:

> Biologists of the time knew that the eye was a very complex structure, containing many components, such as a lens, retina, tear ducts, ocular muscles and so forth. They knew that if an animal were so unfortunate as to be born without one of the components, the result would be severe loss of vision or outright blindness. So they doubted that such a system could be put together in the many steps required by natural selection.[6]

Darwin was aware of the problems the eye posed to his theory. In a personal letter he stated bluntly, "The eye to this day gives me a cold shudder."[7]

Why was Darwin so bothered by the eye? The design of the eye causes problems for evolutionary theory because it is *irreducibly complex.*

While the term sounds daunting, it represents a fairly simple concept. An irreducibly complex system is a "single system which is composed of several well-matched, interacting parts that contribute to the basic function, and where the removal of any one of the parts causes the system to effectively cease functioning."[8]

AN ALL-OR-NOTHING MOUSETRAP

Behe offers a simple illustration of an irreducibly complex system—a common mousetrap.

> The mousetrap that one buys at the hardware store generally has a wooden platform to which all the other parts are attached. It also has a spring with extended ends, one of which presses against the platform, the other against a metal part called the hammer, which actually does the job of squashing the mouse. When one presses the hammer down, it has to be stabilized in that position until the mouse comes along, and that is the job of the holding bar. The end of the holding bar itself has to be stabilized, so it is placed into a metal piece called the catch.[9]

> Behe then asks: How effective will the trap be if it's missing the spring? The hammer? The platform? Behe's answer: It won't catch anything! If *one* piece of the trap is missing, then it won't perform at all. Yet evolution would seem to claim that the mousetrap could evolve slowly, step by step. Thus you would start with a platform, then a hammer, then a spring, and so on. Here's the problem: according to Darwin, each piece of the mousetrap must be useful in and of itself in performing its function. If the purpose of a mousetrap is to catch mice, then what good is a block of wood (platform) or an isolated spring?[10]

This same line of thinking concerning the mousetrap can be applied to the eye. What good is a retina by itself? Or ocular muscles without a lens? As an irreducibly complex system, the eye must come as a package deal or it wouldn't be useful. Yet, according to Darwin, the eye could not come as a package. If it did, it would violate the criteria he established for his theory.

While Behe's mousetrap illustration is well crafted, it could evoke a tepid response from your friend. "Okay, a partial mousetrap wouldn't catch mice. So what?" The following illustration puts your friend into the seat of a malfunctioning Boeing 747 and asks him or her to consider the importance of an irreducibly complex system at thirty-two thousand feet.

An All-or-Nothing Boeing 747

In a magazine article Larry Chapman recalls,

> Looking down at Greenland from 32,000 feet on my trip from Rome to Seattle, I heard an unfamiliar noise in the aircraft that disturbed my slumber. Suddenly I began to wonder what would happen if one tiny part on the enormous Boeing 747 failed. Engines, hydraulics, air pressure—all were complex

DIGGING DEEPER

The design argument is often presented as an argument from analogy that operates like this: (1) Living organisms (human eye, heart, ear, brain) are a lot like machines (camera, pump, loudspeaker, computer). (2) In our experience machines are always designed by an intelligence with a clear purpose for the machine. Therefore (3) living organisms are most likely designed by a mind as well.

The crucial questions for any argument by analogy are these: Are the two objects of comparison a great deal like each other, at least enough to offset the ways they are different? Are the two objects of comparison like each other in ways relevant to the analogy being used? Obviously, supporters of the argument from analogy try to strengthen the analogy (an eye really is like a telescope), while skeptics try to weaken the analogy or offer a competing analogy contradicting the Christian worldview.

systems that worked only when several interdependent parts functioned properly. In vain I sought comfort in my airline pretzels, but comfort can never be found in low-fat foods. I kept thinking of all those dedicated employees (excuse me: "members of the Boeing family") shown on the commercials who apparently love nothing more in life than a well-oiled 747 and who perpetually ponder my safety. But the nagging thought still popped into my head: "Just one faulty or missing part and I'd become the first bomb ever to be dropped on Greenland." In one sense, biological systems are like my Boeing 747: one missing or defective part and they won't work. Here lies one of the major problems that Darwin himself was troubled about. How did highly complex, interdependent biological systems like the eye develop slowly over eons of time? They would never have worked until fully developed.[11]

When you finish sharing one or both of these illustrations, bring your friend back to Darwin's criteria for judging his theory. Darwin said, "If it could be demonstrated that any complex organ existed which could not possibly have been formed by numerous, successive, slight modifications, my theory would absolutely break down." Ask the listener if, after all you've considered, he or she thinks the eye is complex enough to break Darwin's system. And if Darwin's theory is significantly weakened, then what alternative is there?

The Scriptures offer a powerful alternative to Darwin. In Psalm 139, David compares God's design of the human body to a skilled weaver piecing together an intricate basket. "You created my inmost being; you knit me together in my mother's womb" (Ps 139:13). The creation of his frame, psyche and soul cause David to proclaim that he was "fearfully and wonderfully made" (Ps 139:14).

The great preacher C. H. Spurgeon shared David's awe of the human body. He wrote, "We are so wonderfully made, that our organization infinitely surpasses in skill, contrivance, design, and adaptation of means to an end, the most curious and complicated piece of mechanism, not only ever executed by "art and man's device," but ever conceived by human imagination."[12]

The human body is not God's only masterpiece. In the next chapter we'll consider the design and complexity of our home—earth.

11

Are We an Accident? (Part 2)

If the Earth took more than twenty-four hours to rotate, temperatures on our planet would be too extreme between sunrise and sunset for life to exist.

If the rotation of Earth were slightly shorter, wind would move at a dangerous velocity.

If the oxygen level on our planet were slightly less, we would suffocate; if it were slightly more, fires would erupt spontaneously.

What is the best explanation of the remarkable facts that reveal Earth as a place that's just right for life to exist? Is our planet a product of chance or design? Christians argue that the more we learn about Earth, the more it seems that it was created with us in mind. How can we convince our skeptical friends that our planet, just like our bodies, is the handiwork of God?

We suggest you start, not with Earth, but with the red planet—Mars. Present your friend with an illustration that asks him or her to imagine being a participant on a manned mission to Mars.

LIFE ON MARS

As we write this, Russian scientists are organizing an expedition to Mars that will take place between 2016 and 2020. The mission will include astronauts from Russia, Japan and the United States and will take two years to complete. Eighteen months of the project will be spent just traveling to and from Mars. When the astronauts arrive, what will they find? Signs of life? An environment suitable for humans?

Physicist Robin Collins imagines a scenario in which human space travelers arrive on Mars and find a fully functioning, life-sustaining biosphere. When the astronauts enter the Martian biosphere, they find a panel that controls the environment.

At the control panel they find that all the dials for its environment are set just right for life. The oxygen ratio is perfect; the temperature is seventy degrees; the humidity is fifty percent; there's a system for replenishing the air; there are systems for producing food, generating energy, and disposing of wastes. Each dial has a huge range of possible settings, and you can see if you were to adjust one or more of them just a little bit, the environment would go out of whack and life would be impossible.[1]

Ask your friend to put himself or herself in the boots of these astronauts walking around the biosphere. What conclusion would he or she come to? It must be that the biosphere didn't just happen. The biosphere shows the three signs of design mentioned in the last chapter: forethought, intention and planning. It's obvious that the biosphere is a complex structure created and maintained by Martians. The dials on the control panel are perfectly set to support life. If any of the dials were set slightly different, life would be impossible.

Ask your friend to consider a different scenario. Imagine that Martians travel to Earth to observe our environment. What conclusion do you think these Martian explorers would draw from the following facts?

LIFE ON EARTH

Consider these facts about our amazing planet.

- Earth is the only planet in our solar system in which we can breathe. Attempting to breathe on other planets, such as Mars or Venus, would be instantly fatal.
- If the Earth were merely 1 percent closer to the Sun, the oceans would vaporize, preventing the existence of life. On the other hand, if our planet were just 2 percent farther from the Sun, the oceans would freeze.
- Earth has an abundance of water, which is essential for life.
- Life on Earth survives because the ozone level is within safe range for habitation. However, if the ozone level were much greater, there would be too little UV radiation for adequate plant growth. Yet, if the ozone level were much smaller, there would be too much UV radiation for adequate plant growth, and life would be impossible.[2]

After presenting these facts, ask your listener what conclusions he or she thinks our Martian explorers will come to. As they observe a planet carefully designed and meticulously balanced, will they think it happened by chance? Or will they conclude that someone carefully designed our world just as they designed their biosphere? These Martian explorers will certainly come to the same conclusion as physicist Paul Davies, who argues that the precise structure of our universe leads him to believe that the universe has been "rather carefully thought out" and is "compelling evidence for cosmic design."[3]

Yet if Martians are responsible for setting the controls for their biosphere, who is responsible for the precise conditions that make life on earth possible? "Where were you when I laid the earth's foundation?" God replies to a questioning Job. "Who marked off its dimensions?" (Job 38:4-5). When God created Earth, he perfectly balanced it to support human life.

OBJECTION: GOD'S DESIGN OR CHANCE?

Perhaps during this conversation or at another time your friend may bring up an interesting objection to what you've been discussing. He or she does not disagree that the earth is wonderfully complex or shows clear evidence of design. He or she may simply disagree with how we got here. "Isn't it possible," your friend says, "that we just lucked out and were born on the only planet in the universe that could sustain life?"

The objection would be amusing if it didn't have some very smart people agreeing with it. One such individual is Nobel Laureate George Wald, who wrote in *Scientific American*, "Given so

DIGGING DEEPER

The design argument can be understood as an example of what philosophers call an inference to the best explanation. In an argument of this sort a wide range of facts presents itself as a riddle or problem to be solved. After pondering these facts, a hypothesis may suggest itself as one that most adequately explains the facts and solves the riddle. For example, suppose I get a terrible stomachache. Then I recall that I just ate a gallon of ice cream, two bags of popcorn and some candy. A hypothesis suggests itself as the best explanation of the stomachache—it arose because of what I have just eaten. Other hypotheses may also suggest themselves, but I should adopt the explanation that best explains the facts.

However, when it comes to taking this approach with the origin of the universe, be warned! Non-Christian thinkers also use the inference to the best explanation argument and come up with distinctly different explanations. Today many scientists, mathematicians and philosophers consider the design in our world and yet conclude that the theory of evolution, or the idea that design happened by chance, is a better explanation than the existence of an intelligent Designer.

much time the 'impossible' becomes the possible, the possible probable, and the probable virtually certain. One has only to wait: time itself performs the miracles."[4] On the surface such a conclusion makes sense. After all, given enough time *anything* can happen. Against all odds, after billions and billions of years, our universe popped into existence and life surfaced on our lone planet. We won the cosmic lottery!

How should you respond?

We suggest you consider using a communication technique called *feedforward*. This technique involves helping a person understand the logical conclusions that his or her beliefs entail. It's one thing to argue that the overwhelming appearance of design in our world happened by chance; it's another thing entirely to argue that design just happens in other situations. When looking at a painting or flowers arranged in a garden, we never think it just happened. Rather, we compliment the artist or gardener. The same is true of space rockets and moon launches.

SPACE ROCKET—LUCK OR DESIGN?

Philosopher Peter Kreeft envisions two scientists having an interesting conversation after NASA's first moon launch.

When the first moon rocket took off from Cape Canaveral, two U.S. scientists stood watching it, side by side. One was a believer, the other an unbeliever. The believer said, "Isn't it wonderful that our rocket is going to hit the moon by chance?" The unbeliever objected, "What do you mean, chance? We put millions of man hours of design into that rocket." "Oh," said the believer, "you don't think chance is

> a good explanation for the rocket? Then why do you think
> it's a good explanation for the universe? There's much
> more design in a universe than a rocket. We can design a
> rocket, but we couldn't design a whole universe. I wonder
> who can?"[5]

The Christian scientist in Kreeft's illustration does a great job of feedforwarding his unbelieving friend's thoughts to their logical conclusion—universes just happen, while space rockets are the result of intention, forethought and meticulous planning.

A MIND-BLOWING NUMBER

The next illustration tackles the chance objection from a different angle—the visual. You learn more from your sense of sight than from all the other four senses combined. It has been estimated that more than 80 percent of all information comes to you through sight. For an argument or illustration to make sense, one has to literally *see* it. Consider using the following illustration to show a person how unlikely it is that our world and universe happened by chance. The following illustration entails a little math and a lot of doodling.

WHAT'S IN A NUMBER?

Ask your friend what he or she thinks are the odds that our universe, with all its perfectly balanced variables, happened by chance. Take a pen and write the following number on a piece of paper or napkin: $10^{10^{(123)}}$. According to Donald Page (a man who has spent his entire career studying the stars), the odds of the universe just happening are roughly one out of $10^{10^{(123)}}$. Unless your friend has a Ph.D. in mathematics, that number will be meaningless to him or her. Here's some context to understand what an astronomical number $10^{10^{(123)}}$ is.

The number of seconds that have occurred since the beginning of the universe is about 10^{18}, which is a ten followed by eighteen zeros. If you wrote that out on a napkin during lunch, it would look like this:

10000000000000000000.

Here's some more context: the number of subatomic particles in the entire universe is about 10^{80}, which is a ten followed by eighty zeros. If you wrote that out, it would be a pretty impressive number:

100000000000000000000000000000000000000000000000000 0000000000000000000000000000000000.

By now your napkin is filled with zeros and your friend's brain is swirling.

Grab a new napkin and start to write the number mentioned by Page. Be forewarned: you won't ever finish it. Why? Because $10^{10^{(123)}}$ would be a ten followed by a billion billion billion zeros repeated a billion billion times.

As you explain to your friend how unimaginable this number is, keep writing zeros as you speak. Tell your friend that if you started writing this number when the universe began, you *still would not* be finished. Soon the napkin would look something like this:

100000000000000000000000000000000000000000000000000
000000000000000000000000000000000000000000000000000
000000000000000000000000000000000000000000000000000
000000000000000000000000000000000000000000000000000
000000000000000000000000000000000000000000000000000
000000000000000000000000000000000000000000000000000
000000000000000000000000000000000000000000000000000
000000000000000000000000000000000000000000000000000
000000000000000000000000000000000000000000000000000
000000000000000000000000000000000000000000000000000
000000000000000000000000000000000000000000000000000

000000000000000000000000000000000000000000000000000000
000000000000000000000000000000000000000000000000000000
00000000000000 (and so on)

Now we understand why Page argues that it is virtually impossible, from a mathematical point of view, for our wonderfully complex world to have happened by chance.[6]

OPENING THE GOD DOOR

If the odds are overwhelmingly stacked against our world's happening by chance (remember your napkin filled with zeros), then why do some of your coworkers cling to this highly unlikely option? For some, their objections may be lingering questions about the facts you've presented. Others may fear where the admission of an intelligent Designer will lead them. Geneticist Richard Lewontin shares his own opinion about why he and his colleagues reject the idea that our world has been designed by a Higher Power. To acknowledge any force above nature, regardless of signs to the contrary, is to allow "a Divine Foot in the door."[7]

Your friend may have the same fears as Lewontin. To acknowledge the possibility of an intelligent Designer is to also acknowledge the demands that Designer may place on him or her. "At this point," writes Peter Kreeft, "we need a psychological explanation of the atheist rather than a logical explanation of the universe."[8]

WHAT TO MAKE OF A WATCH?

When you and your friend feel like moving on from this issue, we suggest you leave him or her with an illustration that has become synonymous with the argument from design. The illustration is simply referred to as the "watch illustration" and comes from the same man who in the previous chapter compared the human eye to a telescope— William Paley.

Ask your friend to imagine taking a walk.

A WATCH IN THE PATH

In crossing a path, suppose you kick a watch. It's one of those old-fashioned wind-up watches. Even though the back has come off, it's still running. On making a closer inspection, you discover that the watch is a complex system of springs, gears, pinions and bearings that cause it to advance five times a second. If you were to count each part of the watch, you would determine that there are forty-three separate parts that all work in harmony. There is a mainspring to provide power, a set of gears to drive the hour, minute and second hands, and a regulating mechanism to keep the speed of the gears constant. If any of these parts were of a different size or arranged differently, there would be no motion at all. What conclusion would you come to after inspecting the watch? Is it the result of nature, a product of chance or the work of a meticulous craftsman? Common sense would tell us it's the work of skilled watchmaker.

DIGGING DEEPER

Different kinds of design suggest different models of God as Designer:

- *God as engineer (for example, in the order, efficiency and complexity of the world)*
- *God as author (for example, in the information content of DNA)*
- *God as artist (for example, in creating a sunset)*

Paley then makes this observation: Every evidence of design in the watch exists in greater degree in the world of nature. Millions of readers have acknowledged the power of his reasoning and have remembered this lasting illustration.

Interestingly, years before Paley dreamed up his watch illustration, he found an unlikely advocate in the writings of a young French intellectual. Voltaire was an accomplished poet, novelist, scientist and philosopher, and he is still consid-

ered one of France's greatest intellectu-
als. While disparaging Christianity, he
nevertheless reluctantly conceded the
existence of an intelligent Designer.
What convinced him? A watch. Voltaire
wrote: "If a watch proves the existence of
a watchmaker but the universe does not
prove the existence of a great architect,
then I consent to be called a fool."[9]

FURTHER READING

"Back to the Beginning: Glorious Acci-
    dent or Divine Conception?" Y-
    Origins, 2004. For information, see
    www.Y-Origins.com.

* *God as mathematician (for example, in the mathematical character of the world and the different laws that describe it)*

* *God as provider (for example, in the reliability of our senses and intellect for gaining knowledge of the world)*

There is no reason to limit God as Designer. All of these models capture different aspects of what Christians mean when they claim God as Designer.

Davis, Jimmy, and Harry Poe. *Designer Universe: Intelligent Design and the Existence of God.* Nashville: Broadman & Holman, 2002.

Johnson, Phillip. *Darwin on Trial.* 2nd ed. Downers Grove, Ill.: InterVarsity Press, 1993.

Moreland, J. P. *Christianity and the Nature of Science.* Grand Rapids: Baker, 1989.

Final Thought

The Dangers of Agenda Anxiety

Let's be honest: most of us struggle with guilt at having not said more concerning spiritual issues with friends and family, and we may desire to relieve that guilt by telling friends everything we know about God, the Bible and our faith when given the chance. That is, most of us suffer from what one writer described as "agenda anxiety"—the overwhelming anxiety to "get across all points" of a subject regardless of the spiritual state of the person with whom we are speaking.[1]

The book you've just read could easily fuel agenda anxiety. The danger in reading a book filled with illustrations is that you may be tempted to share all of them during one conversation and thus overwhelm a friend or coworker. When sharing your faith, though, the goal is not to create a mental checklist of illustrations and check each one off during a conversation. The goal is to engage your friend in a conversation where the two of you can exchange and consider ideas.

Before any of us share the illustrations in this book, we should all do one thing first: listen. Proverbs 18:13 states, "He who answers before listening—that is his folly and his shame." Why is listening crucial? Because to neglect it is to respond to a person in both folly (speaking out of ignorance) and shame (treating the person as an inferior). Rather than talking prematurely, the wise conversationalist knows that "good understanding wins favor" (Prov 13:15).

The importance of listening cannot be overstated. Before you respond to a person, find out exactly what he or she believes. Os Guinness wisely argues that, when presented with a difficult question, "part of the answer initially is to have *no answer*, for the genuine answer counts only if we have genuinely listened *first*."[2]

If we want our friends and neighbors to listen to our story, then we must listen to theirs. If we want others to attend to our convictions, then we must first attend to theirs. If we desire for others to cultivate common ground with us, we must do so first. In doing so we will create a communication climate in which we can fulfill our deepest longing—having the God conversation with those who matter most.

Notes

Chapter 1: The Power of Illustrations
[1]Quoted in "Illustrations," *Communication Center* notes, 1985.
[2]R. W. Dale, *Nine Lectures on Preaching* (New York: Hodder & Stoughton, 1902), p. 165.

Chapter 2: Can God Be Good If Terrorists Exist?
[1]Cornelius Plantinga Jr., *Beyond Doubt: Faith-Building Devotions on Questions Christians Ask* (Grand Rapids: Eerdmans, 2002), p. 28.
[2]C. S. Lewis, *A Grief Observed* (New York: Bantam, 1976), p. 4.
[3]Ibid., p. 4.
[4]Jürgen Moltmann, *The Trinity and the Kingdom* (San Francisco: Harper & Row, 1981), p. 47.
[5]The answers and perspectives presented in these two chapters reflect our personal theological and philosophical commitments. We do not claim that ours is the only way to approach the problem of evil. For a different perspective, consider these excellent sources: D. A. Carson, *How Long, O Lord? Reflections on Suffering and Evil* (Grand Rapids: Baker, 1990); and John Feinberg, *The Many Faces of Evil: Theological Systems and the Problem of Evil*, 2nd ed. (Wheaton, Ill.: Crossway, 2004).
[6]Norman Geisler and Ron Brooks, *When Skeptics Ask* (Wheaton, Ill.: Victor, 1990), p. 62.
[7]Jean-Paul Sartre, *Being and Nothingness* (New York: Pocket, 1984), p. 478.
[8]This is not to suggest that God will never set a deadline for ridding the world of evil. John states in Revelation 21 that God will one day usher in a new heaven and earth, judge all evildoers, dwell among his people and "wipe every tear" from the eyes of the righteous (v. 4). Peter tells us that God is not quick to set a deadline for judgment or usher in this new order because he is patient with rebellious humans and does not wish for any to perish but for all to come to repentance (2 Peter 3:9).
[9]J. B. Phillips, *God Our Contemporary* (New York: Macmillan, 1960), p. 89.
[10]C. S. Lewis, *The Problem of Pain* (New York: Macmillan, 1986), p. 93.
[11]Philip Yancey, *Where Is God When It Hurts?* (Grand Rapids: Zondervan, 1977), p. 56.
[12]This illustration was inspired by Cornelius Plantinga, *Beyond Doubt*, pp. 32-33.
[13]Alvin Plantinga, "A Christian Life Partly Lived," in *Philosophers Who Believe*, ed. Kelly James Clark (Downers Grove, Ill.: InterVarsity Press, 1993), p. 72.
[14]William Lane Craig, *No Easy Answers: Finding Hope in Doubt, Failure and Unanswered Prayer* (Chicago: Moody Press, 1990), p. 102.

Chapter 3: Can God Be Good If Terrorists Exist? (Part 2)
[1]Quoted in Mimi Hall, "Testimony: FEMA Chief Slow to Grasp Enormity of Katrina," *USA Today*, October 21, 2005, p. G1.

[2] Quoted in Fann S. Wenner, "Bono's Prayer," *Rolling Stone*, November 3, 2005, p. 62.

[3] Millard J. Erickson, *Christian Theology* (Grand Rapids: Baker, 1985), p. 639.

[4] Robert Lightner, *Heaven for Those Who Can't Believe* (Schaumburg, Ill.: Regular Baptist Press, 1977), pp. 34-42.

[5] John MacArthur, *Safe in the Arms of God: Truth from Heaven About the Death of a Child* (Nashville: Thomas Nelson, 2003), p. 82. MacArthur continues: "A young child is truly incapable of rebellion against God because rebellion against God is rooted in deliberate, willful hatred of God. Speaking through the prophet Isaiah, the Lord said, 'Before the Child shall know to refuse the evil and choose the good, the land that you dread will be forsaken by both her kings' (Isa. 7:16). The Lord was referring to the state of young childhood, a time when a person is incapable of making a willful choice to rebel against God" (pp. 84-85). In clarifying this view Norman Geisler states that persons are accountable (possibly between the ages of four and twelve) when "they are aware of the moral law of God (Rom. 2:15). They are morally accountable when they are old enough to know that they what they do is against the moral law of God" (Norman Geisler, *Baker Encyclopedia of Christian Apologetics* [Grand Rapids: Baker, 1999], p. 364).

[6] Erickson, *Christian Theology*, p. 638.

[7] Ibid., p. 639.

[8] Curt Anderson, "Across U.S., Beating Homeless for 'Sport' Not New," *Orange County Register*, January 20, 2006, p. 21.

[9] Quoted in Randy Newman, *Questioning Evangelism: Engaging People's Hearts the Way Jesus Did* (Grand Rapids: Kregel, 2004), p. 113.

[10] C. Stephen Evans, *Why Believe? Reason and Mystery as Pointers to God* (Grand Rapids: Eerdmans, 1996), p. 102.

[11] Philip Yancey, *Disappointment with God* (Grand Rapids: Zondervan, 1988), p. 64.

[12] Alvin Plantinga, "A Christian Life Partly Lived," in *Philosophers Who Believe*, ed. Kelly James Clark (Downers Grove, Ill.: InterVarsity Press, 1993), p. 72.

[13] Quoted in Allen G. Breed, "Miners Wrote Farewell Messages," *Boston Globe*, January 6, 2006; see <www.boston.com/news/nation/articles/2006/01/06/miners_wrote_farewell_messages>.

Chapter 4: Jesus, Buddha or Muhammad?

[1] Cited in James L. Garlow, *A Christian's Response to Islam* (Colorado Springs: Victor, 2005), p. 14.

[2] Ron Rhodes, *Reasoning from the Scriptures with Muslims* (Eugene, Ore.: Harvest House, 2002), p. 7.

[3] Based on the 2001 American Religious Identity Survey (ARIS), Graduate Center, City University of New York; see <www.gc.cuny.edu/faculty/research_briefs/aris/aris_index.htm>.

[4] Based on 2002 statistics from the United States Center for World Missions; see <www.uscwm.org>.

[5] John Stott, *The Contemporary Christian* (Downers Grove, Ill.: InterVarsity Press, 1992), p. 298.

[6] S. Radhakrishnan, *The Hindu View of Life* (New York: Macmillan, 1974), pp. 28-35.

[7]"Religious Groups Sign Ethics Agreement," *Raleigh News and Observer*, September 2, 1993, p. 1C.

[8]Some Hindus believe there is a nonpersonal supreme being (Brahman) that manifests itself through thousands of gods and goddesses. This view would still contradict Muslim, Buddhist, Jewish and Christian claims about God.

[9]The Christian doctrine of the Trinity directly contradicts Muslim teaching (Sura 19:34-35). For Muslims, believing in the Trinity amounts to worshiping other gods, which is strictly forbidden. The notion that Christ is God also contradicts core beliefs found in Judaism.

[10]Michael Green alludes to the maze concept in *But Don't All Religions Lead to God?* (Grand Rapids: Baker, 2002).

[11]Philip Yancey, *Open Windows* (Nashville: Thomas Nelson, 1985), p. 197.

[12]A key difference between Christians and Muslims is that followers of Christ are commanded to care for the needy both inside and outside the Christian community. Muslims are commanded to care only for those inside the Muslim community.

[13]Peter Kreeft, *Making Sense out of Suffering* (Ann Arbor, Mich.: Servant, 1986), p. 1.

[14]Kreeft writes, "I cannot help viewing Nirvana as spiritual euthanasia, killing the patient (the self, the I, the ego) to cure the disease (egotism, selfishness). Buddhism eliminates the I that hates and suffers, yes; but that is also the I that loves" (ibid., p. 4).

[15]C. S. Lewis, *The Four Loves* (New York: Harcourt Brace Jovanovich, 1960), p. 96.

[16]John Wesley, *A Plain Account of Christian Perfection* (1777; reprint, London: Epworth Press, 1952), p. 87.

[17]Jim Beverly, "Buddhism's Guru," *Christianity Today*, June 11, 2001, pp. 69-70.

[18]Norman Anderson, *The World's Religions* (Grand Rapids: Eerdmans, 1975), p. 174.

[19]"Bono: Grace over Karma," book excerpt; see <www.christianitytoday.com/music/interviews/2005/bono-0805.html>.

[20]Beverly, "Buddhism's Guru," p. 71.

[21]Quoted in Lorraine Orris, *Islam 101: Reaching Out with Understanding* (Peachtree City, Ga.: New Life, 2004), pp. 76-79.

[22]David Clark, "Religious Pluralism and Christian Exclusivism," in *To Everyone an Answer,* ed. Francis J. Beckwith, William Lane Craig and J. P. Moreland (Downers Grove, Ill.: InterVarsity Press, 2004), p. 304.

[23]Ibid., p. 305.

[24]Jerry Adler, "Spirituality in America," *Newsweek*, August 29–September 5, 2005, p. 48.

[25]John Berthrong, *The Divine Deli: Religious Identity in the North American Cultural Mosaic* (Maryknoll, NY: Orbis, 1999), p. 15.

[26]Anh Do, "Dalai Lama's Message Universal," *Orange County Register*, local edition, September 22, 2006, p. 2.

[27]Anna Weggel, "Buffet Meals Linked to Weight Gain," *Minnesota Daily*, October 29, 2004, p. 1D.

Chapter 5: Jesus, Buddha or Muhammad? (Part 2)

[1]Richard Spencer, "Millions All over China Convert to Christianity," *Washington Times,* August 3, 2005, pp. A1, A11.

[2]The Qur'an acknowledges Christ's virgin birth, sinless life, ability to perform miracles and status among prophets of Allah. However, it firmly denies the deity of Christ (Sura 5:78), his death (Sura 4:157) and—by implication—his resurrection.

[3]Today the most popular way to get around these three options is to argue that Jesus never claimed to be God—all claims to deity are the result of legend gradually seeping into the biblical texts. We will discuss this objection in detail when considering the resurrection.

[4]C. S. Lewis, *Mere Christianity* (New York: Macmillan, 1984), p. 41.

[5]John Shelby Spong, *Why Christianity Must Change or Die: A Bishop Speaks to Believers in Exile* (San Francisco: HarperSanFrancisco, 1998).

[6]Quoted in K. Campbell, *Man Cannot Speak for Her: Key Texts of the Early Feminists* (New York: Greenwood, 1989), p. 34.

[7]Consider supplementing your study of the Scriptures with the following: Millard Erickson, *How Shall They Be Saved? The Destiny of Those Who Do Not Hear of Jesus* (Grand Rapids: Baker, 1996); Norman Anderson, "A Christian Response to Comparative Religion," in *The World Religions,* ed. Norman Anderson (Grand Rapids: Eerdmans, 1975), pp. 228-37; Ravi Zacharias, "It's Offensive to Claim Jesus Is the Only Way to God," in Lee Strobel, *The Case for Faith* (Grand Rapids: Zondervan, 2000), pp. 145-67.

[8]Millard Erickson offers a thorough overview and critique of differing positions in *How Shall They Be Saved?*

[9]American Bar Association Model Code of Judiciary Conduct, May 2004. To read the entire document go to the American Bar Association website (www.abanet.org) and search "Code of judiciary conduct."

[10]Material taken from Walter A. Elwell, ed., *Evangelical Dictionary of Theology* (Grand Rapids: Baker, 1984), pp. 953-54.

[11]David L. Edwards and John Stott, *Evangelical Essentials* (Downers Grove, Ill.: InterVarsity Press, 1989), pp. 323-24.

Chapter 6: The Resurrection

[1]William Lane Craig writes, "There are really two avenues to a knowledge of the fact of the resurrection: the avenue of the Spirit and the avenue of historical inquiry. The former provides a spiritual certainty of the resurrection, whereas the latter provides a rational certainty of the resurrection" (*The Son Rises* [Eugene, Ore.: Wipf & Stock, 1981], p. 8).

[2]For further study of the church tradition surrounding the deaths of the apostles see: W. H. C. Frend, *Martyrdom and Persecution in the Early Church* (Grand Rapids: Baker, 1981); Paul Maier, *Eusebius—The Church History: A New Translation with Commentary* (Grand Rapids: Kregel, 1999); Herbert Workman, *Persecution in the Early Church* (New York: Oxford University Press, 1980).

[3]Quoted in Craig, *Son Rises,* p. 24.

[4]www.usatoday.com/news/education/2007-04-26-mit-admissions-dean-out_N.htm

[5]While Mark is not one of the original disciples, church tradition teaches that Peter stands behind Mark's Gospel.

[6]*Oprah Winfrey Show,* January 16, 2006.

[7]"The Man Who Conned Oprah," Smoking Gun, January 8, 2006; see <www.thesmoking gun.com/jamesfrey/0104061jamesfrey1.htm>.

Chapter 7: The Resurrection (Part 2)

[1]William Lane Craig, *Resonable Faith* (Wheaton, Ill.: Crossway, 1984), p. 275.

[2]We are indebted to Dr. Gregory Boyd for these observations.

[3]Stein argues that most scholars date Christ's death at A.D. 30. Robert Stein, *Jesus the Messiah: A Survey of the Life of Christ* (Downers Grove, Ill.: InterVarsity Press, 1996), pp. 59-60.

[4]Amy Dorsett, "Crockett Legend Dies Hard," *Raleigh News & Observer*, March 31, 2004, p. 13E.

[5]Jeff Long, *Duel of Eagles: The Mexican and U.S. Fight for the Alamo* (New York: Quill William Morrow, 1990).

[6]The dating of the Gospel of John is a complex issue beyond the scope of this chapter. For an excellent discussion of issues surrounding John see Craig Blomberg, *The Historical Reliability of John's Gospel: Issues and Commentary* (Downers Grove, Ill.: InterVarsity Press, 2001).

[7]For a detailed argument of an early dating of Acts see Colin J. Hemer and Conrad Gempf, eds., *The Book of Acts: The Setting of Hellenistic History* (Winona Lake, Ind.: Eisenbrauns, 1990), pp. 365-410. Hemer settles on an early date of A.D. 62 (p. 408).

[8]The idea for this illustration came from Norman Geisler and Frank Turek, *I Don't Have Enough Faith to Be an Atheist* (Wheaton, Ill.: Crossway, 2004), p. 238.

[9]Ibid.

[10]Jonathan Darman, "The Wrath of Oprah," *Newsweek*, February 6, 2006, p. 42.

[11]Charles Colson, *A Dangerous Grace* (Dallas: Word, 1994), p. 81.

[12]Ibid., p. 82.

Chapter 8: What Would Machiavelli Do?

[1]Stanley Bing, *What Would Machiavelli Do? The Ends Justify the Meanness* (New York: HarperCollins, 2000), p. 78.

[2]Josh McDowell and Thomas Williams, *In Search of Certainty* (Wheaton, Ill.: Tyndale, 2003), p. 46.

[3]The idea for this illustration comes from Francis Beckwith and Gregory Koukl, *Relativism: Feet Firmly Planted in Mid-Air* (Grand Rapids: Baker, 1998).

[4]John Keegan, "How Hitler Could Have Won the War," in *What If? The World's Foremost Military Historians Imagine What Might Have Been,* ed. Robert Crowley (New York: Berkley, 2000), pp. 295-305.

[5]Norman Geisler and Frank Turek, *I Don't Have Enough Faith to Be an Atheist* (Wheaton, Ill.: Crossway, 2004), p. 175.

[6]John Hane, "Three Bosnian Serbs on Trial on Charges of Running 'Rape Factories,' " *Raleigh News & Observer*, March 21, 2000, p. 7A.

[7]Beckwith and Koukl, *Relativism*, p. 23.

[8]J. Budziszewski, *Written on the Heart: The Case for Natural Law* (Downers Grove, Ill.: InterVarsity Press, 1997), p. 171.

[9]For a full transcript of the debate, see <www.renewamerica.us/archives/speeches/ 00_09_27debate.htm>.

[10]John Healy, Amnesty International fundraising letter, 1991. Quoted in William Lane Craig and Walter Sinnott-Armstrong, *God? The Great Debate* (New York: Oxford University Press, 2004), p. 18.

[11]Paul Kurtz, *Forbidden Fruit* (Buffalo, N.Y.: Prometheus, 1988), p. 65.

[12]McDowell and Williams, *In Search of Certainty*, p. 53.

[13]John Warwick Montgomery, *The Law Above the Law: Why the Law Needs Biblical Foundations* (Minneapolis: Dimension, 1975), pp. 22-24.

[14]Richard. L. Rubenstein, review of *Morality After Auschwitz: The Radical Challenge of the Nazi Ethic*, by Peter J. Haas, *Journal of the American Academy of Religion* 60 (1992): 158-9.

[15]Quoted in Geisler and Turek, *I Don't Have Enough Faith*, p. 189.

[16]Montgomery, *Law Above the Law*, p. 24.

Chapter 9: What Would Machiavelli Do? (Part 2)

[1]Os Guinness, *Time for Truth: Living Free in a World of Lies, Hype & Spin* (Grand Rapids: Baker, 2000), p. 103.

[2]Francis Beckwith and Gregory Koukl, *Relativism: Feet Firmly Planted in Mid-Air* (Grand Rapids: Baker, 1998), p. 56.

[3]Ibid.

[4]C. S. Lewis, *Mere Christianity* (New York: Macmillan, 1960), p. 21.

[5]Ibid., p. 19.

[6]Quoted in Os Guinness, *Unspeakable: Facing Up to Evil in an Age of Genocide and Terror* (San Francisco: HarperCollins, 2005), p. 37.

[7]Lewis, *Mere Christianity*, p. 31.

[8]C. Stephen Evans, *Why Believe? Reason and Mystery as Pointers to God* (Grand Rapids: Eerdmans, 1996), p. 43.

[9]Quoted in Paul Rogat Loeb, *Soul of a Citizen: Living with Conviction in a Cynical Time* (New York: St. Martin's Griffin, 1999), p. 14.

[10]Martin Luther King, "Letter from a Birmingham City Jail," in *The World Treasury of Modern Religious Thought*, ed. Jaroslav Pelikan (Boston: Little, Brown, 1990), p. 611.

[11]An extended version of this illustration is found in Guinness, *Time for Truth*, pp. 21-23.

[12]Stanley Bing, *What Would Machiavelli Do? The Ends Justify the Meanness* (New York: HarperCollins, 2000), p. 117.

Chapter 10: Are We an Accident?

[1]Claudia Wallis, "Evolution Wars," *Time*, August 15, 2005, p. 27.

[2]William Paley, *Natural Theology* (1802; reprint, New York: Oxford University Press, 2006), pp. 8-16.

[3]C. Stephen Evans, *Why Believe? Reason and Mystery as Pointers to God* (Grand Rapids: Eerdmans, 1996), p. 37.

[4]Roger Fisher and William Ury, *Getting to Yes: Negotiating Agreement Without Giving In* (New York: Penguin, 1991), p. 27.

[5]Charles Darwin, *On the Origin of the Species* (1876; reprint, New York: New York University Press, 1988), p. 151.

[6]Michael J. Behe, "Evidence for Design at the Foundation of Life," in *Science and Evidence for Design in the Universe*, ed. Michael Behe, William Dembski and Stephen Meyer (San Francisco: Ignatius, 2000), p. 119.

[7]Charles Darwin, *The Life and Letters of Charles Darwin*, ed. F. Darwin (London: John Murray, 1888), 2:273.

[8]Behe, "Evidence for Design," p. 119.

[9]Ibid.

[10]Behe writes, "For example, if we wanted to evolve a mousetrap, where would we start? Could we start with just the platform and hope to catch a few mice rather inefficiently? Then add the other pieces one at a time, steadily improving the whole apparatus? No, of course we cannot do that, because the mousetrap does not work at all until it is essentially completely assembled" (ibid., p. 120).

[11]Rick James, "The Problem with Half an Eye," *Y-Origins*, 2004, p. 39.

[12]C. H. Spurgeon, *The Treasury of David: Psalms 111–150* (Grand Rapids: Zondervan, 1968), p. 279.

Chapter 11: Are We an Accident? (Part 2)

[1]Robin Collins, "The Evidence of Physics: The Cosmos on a Razor's Edge," in Lee Strobel, *The Case for a Creator: A Journalist Investigates Scientific Evidence That Points to God* (Grand Rapids: Zondervan, 2004), p. 130.

[2]Taken from Larry Chapman, Rick James and Eric Stanford, "What Are the Odds?" *Y-Origins*, 2004, p. 21.

[3]Quoted in J. P. Moreland and Kai Nielsen, *Does God Exist? The Great Debate* (Nashville: Thomas Nelson, 1990), p. 35.

[4]Quoted in Gerald Schroeder, *The Science of God: The Convergence of Scientific and Biblical Wisdom* (New York: Broadway Books, 1997), p. 83.

[5]Peter Kreeft, *Fundamentals of the Faith: Essays in Christian Apologetics* (San Francisco: Ignatius, 1988), p. 25.

[6]The idea for this illustration came from a debate between William Lane Craig and Quentin Smith. For a full transcript of the debate, see <www.leaderu.com/offices/billcraig/docs/craig-smith_harvard00.html>.

[7]Quoted in Josh McDowell and Thomas Williams, *In Search of Certainty* (Wheaton, Ill.: Tyndale, 2003), p. 113.

[8]Kreeft, *Fundamentals of the Faith*, p. 26.

[9]Quoted in Walter Elwell, ed., *Evangelical Dictionary of Theology* (Grand Rapids: Baker, 1984), p. 449.

Final Thought

[1]Reuel Howe, *The Miracle of Dialogue* (New York: Seabury, 1963), p. 30.

[2]Os Guinness, *Doubt* (Downers Grove, Ill.: InterVarsity Press, 1976), p. 43.

Name Index

Subject Index